Warwick County, Virginia

The 1643 Church on Baker's Neck and the Genealogy of Neighbor Matthew Jones

Second, Revised and Expanded Edition

By Richard Dunn

CLEARFIELD

Table of Contents

Table of Contents   i
General Foreword   iii

The Sacred & The Secular

Part I, The Second Mulberry Island Church

Documentary evidence 1
Neighboring families...2
Destruction 2
Denomination 2
Other documents... 3
Jones thoughts..4
Mulberry Island churches 4
Archaeology 4

Part II

The MJH 5
    The MJH land & ownership.. 6
    The MJH today.. 7
    The last Jones Owner, Henry Francis Jones................................... 7
The Mill..9

Part III
Matthew Jones Family History, Fact & Belief

Foreword, editorial abbreviations, etc............................10
Matthew Jones I, Origin and birth...................................13
    Timeline..13
    Area of Residence..14
    The Person...16
    Chen..16
    Matt II...17

Nathaniel Ridley/Elizabeth Day Ridley............................18
A Chain of wills (Matt II, Servant, Allen, William):
The Will of MJ II – 1727...20
The Will of Servant Jones -- 1773 22
The Will of Allen Jones--1787 24
The Will of Wm Jones – 1824 24
Allen (and mentions)..26
Ships...29
Matt Jones III & IV (and mentions)...30
       Related or Unrelated   30
The Tingnall Family...36
Francis...37
       At Court   38
       Relationship with the Tingnalls   39
The chen of Francis Jones II & Mary Tingnal..............................39
Ships again..41
The 13 Chen of Francis Jones [III] & Mary Ridley........................41
       The will of Francis Jones III   42
       Info of Dr. Barry Hayes   43
       FJ Related or unrelated   43
Francis Albridgton..46
       F.A.J. Related or Unrelated   47
Albridgton..47
       The 1717 will of AJ   48
       Other Albridgtons, Related and Unrelated   49
       Military   53
Nathaniel..54.
       Related or Unrelated   54
John..56
       Lucas and Southall   59
       Related or Unrelated   62
Servant...64.
       Sons of The American Revolution app.   67
       Related or Unrelated   68
Vincler 74
       Related or Unrelated   75
Briggs and Joneses...77

Harwood..78
    Guardianship   78
    Marriage, Death, Parentage   79
    Related or unrelated   80
Tignal 81
    The 9 chen of Tignal Jones & Penelope Cain......................83
    Related or Unrelated 85
Redding..94
Fanning..94
William 94

Appendix 1: Wake Court Records..96
Appendix 2: Whitaker Charts..99
Appendix 3: CWD Chart..101
Appendix 4: White Plains/Crabtree Creek 110
Appendix 5: Maps...113
Bibliography...114
Index of Names... 119

General Foreword

Religious and secular life in the dim colonial history of Warwick County is partially illuminated by a glimpse of early church activity and by a probing look at the history of the Matthew Jones family of Mulberry Island – a family much involved in secular county matters throughout colonial times and early statehood.

Part I: **The Second Mulberry Island Parish Church (of 1643) and its Social Impact**

A community's primary focus upon the local church as the social center of their community was much more pronounced in the seventeenth century than it is today. There were scarcely any places for gatherings except private homes, but attendance at church by all the neighbors was practically guaranteed. Not only was attendance mandated by law, religious belief was strong. Almost every will began with 'In the name of God Amen' and contained a sentence like 'I give and bequeath my soul unto the hands of Almighty God my body to the earth to have Christian burial in sure and sertain hope ...'[1] Certainly the Church was there for worship, weddings, christenings and burials, but the church also had a vital social function; for that we devote our Part I.

We can visualize families arriving in their Sunday best – by boat in the earliest days, on foot, by buggy later (if the path isn't too muddy or rutted). They're early so they can sit around on the benches outside and socialize -- the landowners, wives and young people. The Wills can talk about their ferry and their ordinary (Emmanuel was also a churchwarden for Mulberry Island Parish), later on Matthew Jones can talk about his tobacco harvest, and every neighbor can talk about his or her concerns or engage in a bit of gossip.

That, at least, is a scene we can imagine (on the basis of pretty good evidence). But let's back up a little. The church we're talking about was just outside what is now Ft. Eustis on Dozier Rd., and the colonial neighbors are those who lived in the upper precincts of Mulberry Island Parish.

Documentary Evidence We know these things because existing deeds tell us so. First the land grant of July 1643 to Capt.William Peirce for 360 acres of land called Bakers Neck, near the plantation of Mr. Thomas Harwood called Queen Hithe, and north of the land on which the MJH (Matthew Jones house) stands [pp. 879-880 of land grants at the Library of Virginia {hereafter just 'LVA page'}]. Our second document is the grant deed of December, 1643, to Capt. William Peirce, which contains the comment "Bakers Necke where the church now standeth" [LVA 927]. Clearly the church was built during the months July to December of that year.

Obviously Pierce (as we spell it now) had a church built on his Bakers Neck land without delay. That is clear, but many good researchers, have placed Bakers Neck wrongly on the map. G.C. Mason, who has contributed valuable

---

[1] Quoted from the 1717 will of Albridgton Jones in Dunn:2016

information, erroneously associates Bakers Neck with the earlier Mulberry Island church in the lower precincts. The error of placement is repeated by Arthur Vollertson and apparently also by John Curry and Dick Ivy. If those researchers were around today, they'd undoubtedly want to correct their writings.

The neighboring families would certainly worship at their nearby church and depend on its pastor for christenings, marriages, and funerals. In short, "… the religious beliefs of the colonists and the public role of the church were at the center of their lives." [from Brent Tarter's *The Church of England in Colonial Virginia* in VMBH vol 112, #4, p. 349]. Some names of families living in the upper precincts of Mulberry Island from ca. 1630 to ca. 1830 were **Jones** (whose land included a tract [the MJH] immediately to the south [S by E] of Bakers Neck, **Hurd** [LVA 29], **Iken** [LVA 218], **Ravennett** [LVA 318 & 613-614], **Rolfe** [LVA 59 & 166], **Peirce** [LVA 879-880 & 927], **Pott** [LVA 113], **Filmer** [LVA 360], **Harwood** [LVA 111-112 & 304 etc.], **Nowell** [or Newell] [LVA 260-261], **Avery** [LVA 144-145], **Pyland** [LVA 471], **Hely** [273-274 & 325], **Wills** (or Wells) [LVA 219-221 & 611], **Hubberd** (LVA 187-8), **Atkins** [in 2V1 (Jul 1894 p. 77], **Sanders** [LVA 282?], and **Lucas** [LVA 709].

Destruction A lengthy and very detailed letter from Secretary Ludwell in Virginia to Lord Berkeley concerning a 12-day violent hurricane in 1667 was published in London in the same year; the text of the letter appears in David M. Ludlum's *Early American Hurricanes*. The letter relates how buildings were destroyed, cattle and people drowned in twelve-foot ocean swells, "drowning the whole Country before it", and that "nothing could stand its fury." It is highly likely that such a violent storm would demolish a church as easily as other buildings. We can readily believe that that hurricane explains the statement in the 1669 land grant to John Iken which says "Bakers Neck where the church *formerly* stood" [LVA 218]. See also Dell Upton's *Holy Things and Profane, The Anglican Parish Church in Virginia* (New Haven, Yale Univ. Press, p. 35): "Seventeenth century parish churches were for the most part as fragile as the houses of their parishioners." [Dell Upton is Professor of Architectural History at UC Berkeley.]

The church was evidently rebuilt between 1669 and 1671/2 and was most likely the church known as the "Upper Church" in the 1759-1760 court records of Warwick County.

Denomination   Anglican churches became 'Protestant Episcopal' towards the end of the 18th century, and around 1830 this church was evidently abandoned completely and taken over by a black community. Of the colonial burials in the churchyard we can be reasonably certain of the interment there of Henry Filmer in 1672, James Barret Southall and his wife Frances (Jones) Southall in the late 18th century[2] and Peyton Randolph Southall in 1812.[3] More recent burials and the monuments there were of black folks; they include Rev. Thomas Wright who died in 1890. There are also three small stones marked L.A.W., W.C.M.M., and T.G.W. The earlier white graves do not have any remaining stones or markers.

We note also the information from Frank W. Tyler in the Tyler Collection, Canterbury, Kent, England: "Henry [Filmer] died in 1671 ... and was buried ... in one of the two churches on the Island. Possibly in the church or church yard of the church that was built by Captain William Pierce at Baker's Neck" --a most likely conclusion. He puts the location of Henry Filmer's plantation at approximately that of Felker Army Airfield—close to and N by E of Bakers Neck.

Thomas Nowell's [or Newell's] land grant of 9 Jul 1658 [LVA 260-261] describes the tract as bounded ... southerly with Queen Hive Creek ..." The November 1660 land grant to Robert Pyland,[4] which grants him 250 acres (in the vicinity of Bakers Neck), refers to a "church path" bordering his land.

Other Documents: The archives of the Kent Libraries in England report that £40 was received by churchwardens Robert Hubberd and Emmanuel Wells, on behalf of the vestry of Mulberry Island Parish as a bequest from Henry Filmer, whose will was dated 1672 [1671], "to provide [silver] plate for the communion table of Mulberry Island Parish Church." We note that both Hubberd and Wells [or Wills] resided in the Bakers Neck area[5], and that the bequest of 1671 could only refer to a church which was built after the hurricane of 1667 and after the 1669 comment in Iken's patent. A church destroyed by the hurricane of 1667 and then rebuilt (evidently between 1669 and 1671-2) would be new at the time of Filmer's bequest. Additional research also indicates that a letter from Henry Filmer's nephew Robert Filmer shows, too, that Henry was a resident of this area: " your friend and neighbor Mr. Thomas Nowell at his lodging at Queens Hith" ... [the letter of 13 Aug 1661, from London is in 68W4 (Oct 1960), 408-428; it also cites the

---

[2] He in 1787, she in 1780.
[3] Information from Jay Gaidmore at The College of William and Mary's Swem Library, Special Collections, citing *VMHB*, v. 45, p 285.
[4] LVA land recs 471
[5] Hubberd: "... at the head of Skeathes Creek ... by a N corner tree of Thomas Harwood ..." [LVA land recs 187-8]; Wells [Wills]: "... along the road that goes down to Mulberry Island ... formerly taken up & patented by Tho Ikens ..." [LVA land recs p 220]

3

source, the Kent Libraries. Thomas Nowell's [or Newell's] land grant of 9 Jul 1658 [LVA 260-261] is described above ..."

Jones Thoughts: It is thinkable, but by no means provable, that the Jones component to the York County-Mulberry Island connection is deep. "Rev. James Sclater was minister of Charles Parish in York County from 1688 until 1724 and *"was officiating also in Mulberry Island Parish" [Brydon, 533]*. The records of Charles Parish Vestry (in York County) show the 1712 death of a Matthew Jones. The land of the 18th – century "MJH" (the Matthew Jones House on Mulberry Island) bordered on Bakers Neck immediately to the N by W. "Frances" (and " Francis ") was a frequent name in that line; Frances, John , Wm. B. Jones (who in 1873 granted the land for the nearby Methodist church)[6], and the Matthew Joneses might all have been in the same line of descent and all connected in some way to the churches in or near Bakers Neck. Of possible interest to this Jones idea is the 1824 will of Wm. Jones[7] which gives to his *son* Wm. Jones "my Brick House plantation [,] Queen Hive [,] ..." That document shows that he [Wm. Jones] had by that time (1824) acquired both the Matthew Jones House of c1727 and also the land which earlier belonged to Thomas Harwood.

Mulberry Island Churches: In Dunn: 2008, 3rd ed., are several mentions of Mulberry Island Parish. There was the first church of c1727 in the lower precincts and some pages suggesting sites in the upper precincts of the county (as mentioned in court sessions from 1702 to 1760); these mentions indicate that there was a church in that upper area long after the hurricane of 1667. No court records at all exist from 1643 or 1667, so we cannot expect any court records of the hurricane or the destruction of a church.

Archaeology. Modern archaeology has not found artifacts from colonial times on the site they call 44NN176, but a parallel pair of trenches with an E-W orientation has been found. The trenches correspond to the earlier observations of Maar Associates and G.C. Mason (which report visible foundations). More importantly, the E-W orientation of the main axis of a building, shown in the 2018 inspection, corresponds to ancient ecclesiastical law for the orientation of an Anglican Church (see G. Mason, "The first Colonial Church of Denbigh" in 57VMHB).

Another archaeologist opined that "A church was built there in the 17th-century and then another took its place at the same location in the 19th-century. ... And the level of archaeological work at that location is not

---

[6] Ft. Eustis records—communicated by Dr. Chris McDaid
[7] R. Dunn:2018/72

sufficient to prove or disprove [any] option." Whether the trenches date back to colonial time or to a more recent construction, the contents (probably brick) have been picked clean.

But to return to the social aspect of life around the church we return to Dell Upton's *Holy Things, Profane, The Anglican Church* (op.cit.): 'It was on Sunday morning, of course, that the churchyard really came to life. At mid-morning, the parishioners began to gather in groups, standing or sitting on benches scattered under the trees "for the People to sitt on before Divine Service." Notices were tacked to the church door, as they had been on medieval parish churches ... One dated Sunday Decemr 12th "Pork to be sold tomorrow at 20/ per Hundred." Church-door notices were used to "outlaw" slaves, the Virginia term for legal declarations that a slave had run away. Gentlemen discussed business, and "rings of Beaux" chatted before and after the service.'

The MJH   Inserted below is a computer-generated picture of the MJH in its 1730 configuration. A few words[8] should be added about the MJH (the

Matthew Jones House at Fort Eustis). It is adjacent to Baker's Neck to the SE on Mulberry Island. One of the bricks on the house is inscribed ' Matthew Jones 1727.' It was begun in c1725 as a frame house with earthfast[9] construction (Period 1). In 1730 brick was installed to the frame exterior

---

[8] Taken from the investigation by the William and Mary Center for Archeological Research in 1991.

[9] 'Earthfast' denotes a foundation technique of placing poles into the ground.

walls (Period 2). In 1893 the building was expanded by the new owner, **Rev. Wm. R. Webb,** to a full 2 stories instead of the original 1 ½ stories. In the typed statement by Fannie J. Wright about the "Brick House Farm" she says 'Fa, Henry F. Jones, was born in the little shed rm on N side of hse... From my fa, the Farm passed into the possession of Thos. Tabb of Hampton.". The land of the MJH house with the 1727 plate was an *acquisition* just as the York properties were acquisitions *but not residence* locations of this family in the 17th century. The MJH land might have been purchased by Matthew Jones I from the estate or heirs of **Capt. Wm. Pierce** (whose land appears to have included that area).[10] Pierce d. ante 22 Jun 1647 (/23). It is certain that many members of this Jones family lived and continued to live in the lower end of the county. **Matthew II,** the probable builder of the MJH apparently had an existence divided between Isle of Wight County, where he had established a domicile, and Warwick County where he had the MJH property -- apparently given him by his father. While primogeniture favored another son, **Francis,** it looks like some of the other sons of this family also received land from their father in the vicinity of their original home, which was probably at the lower end of Mulberry Island. McSwain also cites mentions of lands adjoining Fisher's Creek and the **Matthew Jones** tract in 1696 and 1701 (Nugent ... /8 & /42) (McS /174), thus providing further evidence of a residence in the lower precincts of Mulberry Island.

The MJH Land and Ownership   In 1918 the U.S. Government bought lands of Mulberry Island in Warwick County which became known as Ft. Eustis, US Army. The command of the installation is directly in charge of all the properties and operations on the base. The MJH is located on the installation and is accessed from Harrison Road. In the early 1990s, after a *Preservation Plan* was done, Ft. Eustis obtained funds for preservation of the MJH and work was begun -- with Jim Melchor, senior manager with the Corps of Engineers at Norfolk, as Preservation Director.

Effort was made to preserve as much of the original portions of the building as possible. It was decided that the best use of the house was as an architectural museum unto itself, so the interior walls were left unfinished, the roof-line retained its sag, and the cracked beam was left in place—while steel was installed, and many other means and processes applied to preserve the building. APVA named Jim recipient of the Gabriella Page Historic Preservation award for 1995. The Chief of Staff for Ft. Eustis was Col. Shellabarger. The house had undergone three phases of building

---

[10] A record of the December, 1643 patent for the 2100 acres of Pierce has been preserved by the Library of Virginia on p. 927 of land patents.

The initial work was done 1725-1730, Rev. Webb bought the property in the late 19th century and enlarged the house to accommodate his family. That enlargement, Phase III, caused the structural failures described above. Reportedly (by Fannie Jones Wright, b.1873) there was an outside kitchen 40-50' from the house on the S side and it was the brick from this kitchen that Rev. Webb used to enlarge the house.

■■■

Some years after the preservation work, a sewage-water treatment plant that Ft. Eustis had installed on the land west of the MJH was taken out of operation and later removed entirely. Down that same slope, which leads down to the creek, originally was undoubtedly a wharf for loading the cash crop onto a boat—'the brickhouse landing' of many records.

The MJH Today[11] In the early 1990s, work was begun. Today we have a rare example of an early 18th century residence in this country. It's ownership extended through several Jones families (see the chain of wills described below) to public sales in the 19th century and finally to the U,S. Government in the early 20th century. A letter of 14 Apr 1966 from Estelle Webb (Powell) to Col. Ridgell at Ft. Eustis says that her fa was Rev. W. R. Webb (-1909), her mother Mary E. Williams; that her mother sold the farm in 1915 to Emmett Milstead, and "we stayed on until Mr. Milstead sold the place to the Fed. Govt. in 1917.

The last Jones owner of the ' Matthew Jones House' was **Henry Francis Jones**. He was born in the House in 1839[12] (the MJH was then already over 100 years old). Henry was a veteran of the CSA. In 1866 he married **Justinia Neuman** and they lived at 'Shelly'—a nearby plantation on the Warwick River side of Mulberry Island willed to him in 1866 by his mother,[13] **Mary Ann (Wood) Jones**, 2nd wife of **William Servant Jones**. In the same year Hen. Francis m. Justinia ("Jessie") Newman, (-1876); Ms. S.M. Walker, the sis-in-law of Henry Francis, became his housekeeper at Shelly.

---

[11] Warwick County, as it has been known since 1642-3, was first formed in 1634 as 'Warwick River County,' one of the colony's original shires; subsumed by the city of Warwick, then by Newport News in the 1950s.
[12] Historian's office at Ft. Eustis – interview with Fannie.
[13] *Deed Bk I, 67 at Newport News Courthouse*

Henry Francis had interests in a number of real estate and farming ventures;[14] in 1882 he became Inspector for the establishment of oyster beds, in at least 1887 was a trustee for Stanley District Free Schools;[15] he leased a house in NN on 20 Sep 1901 (after the m. of his yngst dau), and he died in NN on 24 Jul 1920. His death certificate lists his occupation as justice of the peace (information partially supplied by his dau Fannie).

The title to the 'Brickhouse Farm' (MJH) traveled from Matthew II (or maybe Matthew I) to William S. Jones Jr., but a Pembroke Jones of Warwick Co.[16] [wife Mary Willis and son of Mary S. Jones (w. 5 Aug 1867 pr. 9 Dec 1880) & fa JJ] reportedly acquired the property in 185--[?] from Miles King & George Fitchett).[17] 'This property had been conveyed by a Special Commissioner to Colonel Thomas Tabb by deed dated 14 Nov 1887, recorded 25 Jan 1888, in *deed book 3, pages 476-477*. The original deed book is in the office of...the Corporation Court, NN, VA.'[18] The existing records seem to indicate that the MJH was sold by William S. Jones Jr..in 1832 then bought again by him, and once more sold. We lack records to clarify all this.

An interview with descendants--from the Historian's Office at Ft. Eustis: An article by Col. Ridgell in the NN Daily Press 7 June 1964.   Interview wi Noah Webb, 85, of Hampton.

> Noah had one son & 3 daus.   [His bro] Robt. has 2 sons. Rev. William d. in 1909. Speaks of bricks believed supplied by Dowsing family, "who for several generations operated a brickyard near the MJH". Calls MJH "Bourbon". Says Webb purchased MJH from C. Tabb in 1882. Says that Mrs. Fannie Jones Wright was then 91, a "gr'grandau of the builder," and that Sarah Webb Fitchett is sis of

---

[14] Including the 13 Dec 1879 sale (Warwick Co. Deed Book 1/580 in NN) of Ft. Crafford 'by **Henry Jones** and **G.W. Fitchett**.' He raised peanuts at Shelley [*lien of 5 Jul 1880 at NN Crthse*] where he kept some of his sheep, c125 hogs, buggies & carts. A deed of 12 Feb 1881 describes it as 225 acres and the residence of HF. , He had land sales in Warwick Co. as late as 27 Mar 1920. (*DB 44/408 & 2JHA3/4*).

[15] Warwick Co. recs at NN Crthse – deed of 27 Jun 1887

[16] *6T48* shows a Pembroke Jones of ECC in 1855 in the Navy.

[17] From records in the NN Crthse concerning property deeds.   JJ had made a deed 15 Aug 1866 to Pembroke & Thomas   Jones.

[18] A letter of 10 Aug 1966 from   George S. DeShazor, Jr., Clerk of the Hustings Court, City of NN, to Mrs McSwain, (photocopied in her book).

Noah [the husb. of Mrs. Noah O. Webb, of NN was Noah. O. Webb; his bro was Robt.].

Certified Copy of deed of 8 Jul 1893 is in *Warwick Co. Deed Bk #12/275:* Thomas Tabb and wife, Virginia, grant to Wm. R. Webb 220 acs in Stanley Dist., Warwick Co., known as "The Brick House", incl "The Queen Hive"...conveyed to Thos. Tabb by deed of J.B. Hubbard bearing date 14 Nov 1887 and recorded in *deed bk. 3/476, Clerk's Office, County Crt of Warwick Co.* Notation in margin says "mailed to atty for Estelle W. Powell, grandau of grantee." ... inherited by her grandfa, William S. Jones. Fa, Henry F. Jones, born in little shed rm on N side of hse. "Matthew, William S. and William B. [Hellcat Billy] and many others [including W.C. Miner, a CSA friend *{Vollertson/317}* were buried ca 100 yds from the hse. Where the graveyard was is now part of an abandoned rr bed." [The gravestones were taken to Lebanon Church {Thanks to Jodie Davis, former Ft. Eustis historian, for this info}].

The Mill   Matthew I owned a mill in York Co. for a short time. Matthew is described as 'merchant' in the deeds [*York Co. Deeds, Orders, W.s* and *Chancery No. 8 (1687-1691) /30-33*] granting him a mill 24 Aug 1687 and 166 acres of land 26 Sep 1687[19].

In the mill-deed, seller **Samuell Snignall** describes himself 'att Charles Parish in York Co.,' and Matthew Jones 'of the Parish of Mulberry Island in Warwick Co.'[*York #8 1687*, #9/13 /1-3]. According to Col. Ridgell, the mill was known as '**Harwood's** Mill.' Evidently the land (and later also the mill) was sold by Matthew to **Henry Hayward** (Dorman, *York Co. Deeds* /8) shows the subsequent sale of the land as 24 Mar 1690/1); a later will[20] by Hayward bequeaths both properties: 'A parcel of woodland containing 1100 odd acres which I bought with the Mill of Matthew Jones to furnish them [i.e. Hayward's heirs] with timber for repairing the Mill ....' McSwain, op. cit. page 176 points out that the price of the mill (£132) was a large sum of money, and that the paucity of land around it (one acre) meant that the mill itself was the important thing. This is the only property of 'our' MJ for which records of sale exist.

---

[19] *Land Patents/579:*   20 Apr 1687   166 a. to S.Snignall

[20] The Hayward w.: Currer-Briggs, *English Adventurers and VA Settlers* /399 cites *York County Records No. 14, 1709-1716*; the will is dated 4 Nov 1711 and was probated 17 Mar 1711/12.

There is no mention of the name 'Harwood' either in the deed of Samuell Snigall or in the rather lengthy will of Henry Hayward. On the contrary, Snignall says:

> for many yeares paste I have been lawfully possessed of [a] certain water mill ... commonly called Pocoson Mill ... which mill and mill house I spend [spent?] to built [build?] and been at great charge in maintaining ....

The mill is also called 'Howard's' in some sources; this is probably a corruption of 'Hayward.' In addition, 'Hayward's Mill' might be more correct than 'Harwood's' as the mill was in the Hayward family for quite a long time (probably 20-30 years or more). See York Wills #14 4 for w. of H. Hayward.

The large sum of £ 132 paid by Matthew for the mill contrasts with the £ 14/4/0 appraisal of the entire estate of George Albrighton (so spelled) in the document from the court session 21 Aug 1697 [McSwain].

There might have been another mill. Dr. Barry Hayes says, "[A] Samuel Browne patented a small plot of 42 acres 'at Waters Creek along Mill Dam' in Warwick Co. ... near the mill that Matthew Jones the Elder had acquired a generation earlier."[21]

Matthew Jones Family History
Fact and Belief
***
Foreword to Part III

The family history of **Matthew Jones** of Mulberry Island and his progeny is a <u>work in progress.</u> Due to the pillage[22] and destruction in the Civil War

---

[21] In *6JHA* (Spring 2000) /4. Part of Dr. Hayes' article 'Dr. Samuel Browne (c1670-1740) and Matthew Jones [II] (c1670/80 -1728) of IoW Co., VA: Brothers-in-Law?'

[22] One example is the letter of a union soldier in 1862: "Dear Brother ... a brick building was used as a kind of County Clerk's office, the records & documents of the County were kept there... I was lucky and got a handful of deeds etc. I have one written 1669. I send you some of them." [VA Counties at Swem Library, Coll. Of William and Mary]

and to fires,[23] there is little documentation in existence for Warwick County -- the main setting of this study. Even post-civil-war records existed at the courthouse in Newport News before the fire there of 1893 (though some remain). But despite all the 19th century destruction of records, available information has actually increased some over time. Just recently (in 2012) the very important 1717 will of **Albridgton Jones,** taken from the records of Warwick County by northern soldiers, was returned to Virginia! Hopefully still more documents will turn up in old chests or attics.

Also many books have come out over time which deal with relevant subjects, and I immodestly include my transcripts of some 1100 pages of existing colonial and early statehood Warwick court documents from eight different repositories around the country. Also, the records of neighboring counties and states are mostly intact (though spotty), there are records of other families, and copies of VA records sent to England. And Ft. Eustis, the College of Wm and Mary, and the Corps of Engineers have provided analyses -- and strengthening in the 1990s -- of the existing 'MJH'.

And we have the valuable works of other researchers—of which I single out those of **Amelia Ann Whitaker** ('AAW') of 1895, of **Camilla Webb Davis** ('CWD') of c1931 and of **Eleanor McSwain** ('McS') of 1984. We have built upon the information of all those works, eliminating errors and adding data. We've applied logic and plausible theories, used details of law and other disciplines, but we still face unanswerable questions due to the lack of records in Warwick Co. and the dearth of 17th and early 18th century records anywhere. This is indeed a work in progress. The effort here is to summarize existing beliefs and facts for the first 250 years of this family history, adding whatever we can. **Whitaker, Davis,** and **McSwain** all extend their research to even later times and later descendants. Indeed the descendancy extends to the present day and covers many parts of the United States with thousands of individuals. This book, however, confines itself to some of the hundreds of individuals in the period late 17th century through the 19th century. Both McSwain and Davis follow some families into the 20th centuries.

For further research, a library like the Library of Virginia in Richmond or the Family History Library in Salt Lake City would be helpful, in addition to such repositories as the State Library of North Carolina and online services like Ancestry.com. One should note that some of the sources cited here are

---

[23] Loose records from 1787 to 1819 burned, the clerk's office in Warwick County was burned on 15 Dec 1864, and the Richmond fire of 3 Apr 1865 destroyed records sent there for protection. [Info from *Lost Records,* The Library of Virginia]

the county record books, others refer to collections of those records—photocopied into collections; generally the individual books are at the counties, the collections in state libraries.

To somewhat simplify the process, I supply *in the text* the page numbers from my transcriptions of all known, existing court records of Warwick County, Virginia in the form (/123). These transcriptions are verbatim copies of the readable records found in the eight repositories; the transcriptions are available at the Library of Virginia (LVA), The Rockefeller Library in Williamsburg, The Family History Library in Salt Lake City, etc.

***

Editorial Factors There were many other Joneses in Warwick County in colonial times: Anthony, Catherine, Herbert, Rice, et al – in immigration records, etc., and there is even a Matthew or two in Warwick County, but I have ignored the Joneses who seem not to be germane to this study. Nugent shows no less than four persons with the name '**Mathew Jones** as having been transported from England in the 17th century: on 10 Oct 1672, 23 Oct 1673, and 26 Apr 1686—those persons being prob inapplicable here.

Symbols and abbreviations (necessary in graphic representations and desirable in such a complicated and extensive study) include: c (circa)=about, /=page, m.=married, b.=born, d.=died or death, w.=will, bu.=buried, ch=child, chen=children, dau=daughter, ex.=executor/trix, fedcen=federal census, bef.=before, pr.=probate, fa=father, info=information, gdn=guardian, orp=orphan, grfa=grandfa, prnts=parents, dsp=died a single person, dyng=died young, pet.=petition, unm=unmarried, fn=footnote, re=regarding, adm.=administrator, NN=Newport News, etc., and the initials of the most popular of the Jones names have been used: .MJ= Matthew Jones, SJ=Servant Jones, TJ=Tignal Jones, HJ=Harwood Jones, JJ=John Jones, AJ=Albridgton Jones and FJ=Francis.

The bibliographical section of this book provides fuller info for all books. In the text, references to **McSwain** are shown as e.g. (McS ...). References to **C.D. Webb** are shown as (CDW ...), and references to the writings of **Amelia Ann Whitaker** are shown as (AAW ...). The titles of other books are also abbreviated in the text or identified by the year of publication.

The main object of this project is to provide an abundance of source material. In the best cases it has been possible to show connections between generations and sometimes a little more information. Where connections were uncertain or not known, the references are placed in a category called

'Related or Unrelated' for the benefit of future researchers. Both the index and the Table of Contents must be consulted in researching individuals.

Many citations refer to *original records*, and some refer to the more recent *collections* of original records. Both are valid. The collections hold photocopies of the original records. The original records are most likely to be found in the counties; the collections are often found in large libraries.

Matthew Jones I who m. Elizabeth Albridgeton.

Origin and Birth As 'Jones' is a very prevalent name in Wales, many secondary or tertiary reports claim Wales to be the country of origin for 'our Matthew Jones,' but there is no compelling evidence of such origin. **McSwain**[24] (McS 172) points out that both Wales and VA have places called Denbeigh –indicating that there were Welsh immigrants in VA. That conclusion would not be disputed; 'our' Matthew could have been born in VA, and that conclusion cannot be disputed either. Few suggest a year of birth for him before 1640, but most researchers favor the years 1640-1650 for good reason. There is now the possibility of identifying the father of 'our' **Matthew Jones**: a **Francis Jones** who d. c1669, and a possible brother, **John**, who lived in I. of W, Co.

Timeline
1640-1650   birth year estimated.
1667 - 1683 m. **Elizabeth Albridgeton**[25]
1674   witness 9 Oct: first known mention in court records Signature of MJ
1678   c15,000 lbs. of tobacco shipped by Matthew Jones (per the Controller of Tonnages and Poundage, London). communicated by Mr. Kneebone, Lib. of VA]
1682: mention of him in Journal of House of Burgesses (McSwain, cites *House of Burgesses* vol.1659– 1693, p. 179 and also cites *6T44.*)

---

[24] See Bibliography
[25] In 1667 the w. of her father **Francis Albridgeton** does not mention Matthew Jones. The 1683 w. of her brother **Richard** does. So we just select a midpoint as an estimate. The m. probably was not performed by **Rev. James Sclater,** who was the 'clerke' of Charles Parish from 1688 (*Brydon, /533*) – a bit late for that m. -- but he could have officiated in the baptisms of Matt's chen. Brydon also points out that Sclater also officiated in Mulberry Island Parish (*see York Co. records and Brydon*).

1687, 26 Sep, Purchases a mill in Pocoson River and land in York County from **Samuel Snigall**   (*York Co. Deeds* No. 8 /30-33)
1688:   court order to appraise an estate with others (Dunn:2016: /2)
1690/91, Mar 24:   resells the mill, land to **Henry Hayward** *(Dorman.../8)*
1699-1705   JP on Warwick County Court (/ 62 [1699]-/198 [1705])
1708 & 9   appt'd. sheriff of Warwick Co. (*McIlwaine III/180*)[26]
1712-1713   died.

Area of Residence The quitrents show Matthew Jones possessing 750 acres in Warwick County in 1704,[27] and in 1713[28] the quantity was 400 for ' **Matthew Jones Sen**ʳ. The appellation 'Senʳ' implies a 'Jr' –a matter of interest when Matthew II is discussed later. The date of 1713 does not necessarily negate the presumed death date of 1712 for Matthew I; the obvious purpose of the quitrent roll is to tally the amounts paid by or due from each landowner to the crown and to show totals; a tract of land continues to exist even if the former possessor had d., and the tax may then be payable by the wife or heir – whenever that matter is resolved.

However, in a court record of 7 May 1713 (/211) , i.e. separate from the rent roll, the name 'Matt. Jones Senʳ' appears, but we still can't be sure of the meaning.   'Jr.' becomes 'Sr.' in the Colonial Period when the older person dies, or else the suffix is just dropped. The terms 'elder' and 'younger' were often used especially if a father-son relationship was not the case. In any event we are faced here with an uncertainty, but all indications make it reasonably clear that the actual death date had to be 1712 or 1713.

The reduction in the number of acres (750 in 1704 down to 400 in 1713) indicates that Matthew had divested himself of 350 acres either by selling some of his land, by selling the entire property and buying another, or possibly by giving land to his sons.   **Francis**   alone (except for the father) had land in Warwick County.

We can speculate that Matthew I personally acquired the land of 'MJH' for the purpose of building a house there, but no records exist to support that idea. Also the size of MJH land might not be shown very precisely, and we do not know the actual area or the borders of that tract. With regard to rent

---

[26] Cognets:1958/4, gives the dates as 28 Apr 1708 and 26 Apr 1709.

[27] The quitrent rolls of 1704 for Warwick Co. are in Cognets:1958 /187 and elsewhere.

[28] The quitrent rolls for 1713 are in the *Blathwayt Papers, Rockefeller Library,* Williamsburg, VA.

payments, it might be useful to note that MJ's **wife Elizabeth** reportedly d. c1697, as she is not mentioned in any known existing records after that (/ 193), Therefore her name could not appear on the tally of rents for any date after that death.

In each year (from at least 1700) lists were made by the magistrates[29] of the 'tithables' (those who would be required to pay a tax *to the county*). Additionally, various persons were appointed 'surveyors' of roads.[30] Both of these kinds of appointments were meted out to persons living in the area assigned to them. So, for example, the **Harwoods** always had assignments in the upper end of the County. Existing records are scant, but the conclusion is clear: most of 'our' Joneses, specifically **Matthew I** and his sons **Francis, Nathaniel,** and **John** and also **Tingnall**, were assigned to the *lower* precincts of Mulberry Island, not to the upper precincts of M.I. as the MJH location might suggest.[31] This is therefore a possible answer to the question of where the family of Matthew Jones with his wife **Elizabeth Albridgton** and their chen lived . It's clear that they did not live in the MJH in their early years. *Nugent* (/118) also says Matthew was adjacent to **John Mallicot, William Rascow,** and **James Floyd** on 29 Oct 1696.

McSwain also cites mentions of lands adjoining Fisher's Creek and the **Matthew Jones** tract in 1696 and 1701 (*Nugent ... /8 & /42*) (her /174), thus providing further evidence of a residence in the lower precincts of Mulberry Island.

McSwain also adds other thoughts: "There are several references about Mathew Jones in <u>York</u> County ... **Mark Seires** brought a suit for debt against Mr. **Henry Andrews** but the suit was dismissed for **Mrs. Elizabeth Jones** intervened, promising Seires' attorney 'her husband's bill of

---

[29] May 1707: 'ye justice appointed to take ye Same.' (/124)

[30] not surveyors in modern parlance but simply persons assigned to remove obstructions and to maintain property (usually roads) as a record shows: 'Ordered that the respective Surveyors of the High Ways ... shall see y^t the high ways are cleaned and y^t they also cause to be filled and lopp all such dead trees as Stand within reach of the road (/193).

[31] One example of the area assignments is 21 May 1701 (/99): 'The List of Tytheables appointed to be taken by the Sev^{ll} Members of the Court as followeth Mr. **Matthew Jones** the Lower Precincts of Mulberry Island, Mr. **John Tingnall** below Water's Creek.' A later example is 1 Mar 1753 (/374): ' **John Jones** Gent is by the Court appointed to take the List of Tithables from Deep Creek to the lower End of this County for the ensuing Year. [This man was sheriff] (/373) -- appt'd 31 Jul 1751 (/624) [Exec. Journal IV/ (349)]. Another example : **Maj. H. Harwood**, upper pcnct;
(Footnotes 32-36 not in use)

exchange for the debt.' The item also mentions a 'shipping for London'. Where was Matthew Jones? ... This information was in the York County Court Minutes of 25 March 1669.* At a Court 24 February 1697 **John Doswell** assignee of **Mathew Jones** was mentioned.* [At an] estate sale of 18 Jun 1689 purchases were made by Mathew Jones with **George Albritton** his security ..." [*Her footnotes cite *Dorman, York Co., VA*, Book 10, Pt 3, p. 80; and *Book 8*, Pt 2, p. 34 respectively.] She continues "... The Church of Charles Parish was in the area known as Pocoson." [her p. 176] McSwain also says that **Matthew's** wife **Elizabeth** was not of age in 1667 because her father's will left his wife and chen 'in trust.' [her p. 177).

The Person of Matthew I   Matthew was a wealthy merchant as evidenced by his large expenditure of £ 132 sterling for the mill[37] and the shipment to London of 15,000 lbs. of tobacco. He also evidently had an ownership in one or more ocean-going ships [38] and evidently was able to pass on to his sons land and wealth—judging from the apparent means the sons had--their ownership of land and ships, and their titles of 'gent' in the records (indicating that they were not workers but landed gentry).

In 1687 **Grace Procer** alleged that Matthew Jones fathered her child (/50), but we don't know if this was 'our' MJ, if the claim was truthful, or what the result of the allegation might have been.

The chen of Matthew Jones [I] and Elizabeth Albridgton:

Some chen might not have lived to maturity, and we do not have the documents we'd like to have in order to name the chen who survived. Among the boys are those whose names are frequent among descendants of **Matthew Jones** and show compelling reasons for inclusion in this family. They were **Francis, Albridgton, Matthew, Nathaniel,** and **John** – as the following will show. The girls probably included Marget (name given to a sister of Matt II in his will of 1727) and **Agatha (or Agethy)** a name appearing as a dau of Matthew II in the same w. and as a dau of Matt II's brother **Albridgton**

No doubt the descendants of the daus of the 'first' family added to the abundance of familiar names as well. The appearance of names in different

---

[37] McSwain /176 notes that that was an enormous sum "At a time when many ... would leave heirs a shilling" and "when tracts of 100 acres of land were sold for [a few] shillings." Indeed the entire estate of **George Albrighton** was valued at £ 14/4/0 in the court session of 21 Aug 1697.
[38] Also McSwain says 'There are several references [in *English Duplicates*) to a ship owner, **Matthew Jones** of London, England in 1700 [her /174].

contexts means that researchers must rely on this table of contents and the name index to research any given person. The chen of the Matthew II families were, **Agatha**, **Britten** (d. aft. 22 Sep 1784), **Ann,** **Marget "} & Servant.**

This part of the genealogy looks like this:

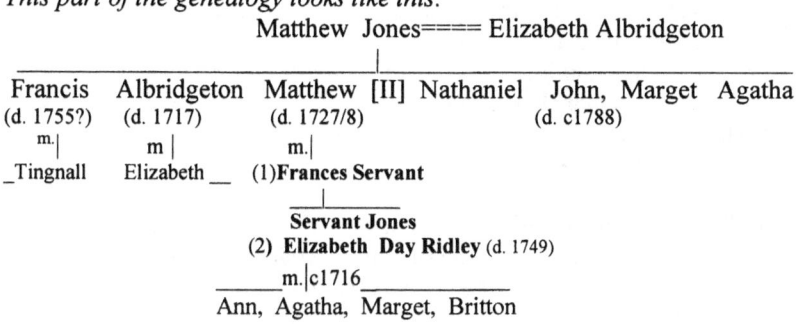

Matthew Jones [II], third son

Matthew II bears the name of his father and was the third son according to the naming pattern. He married (1) Frances Servant, the daughter of Bertrand Servant bef 1716; their son (and evidently the only surviving ch. of that m.)[43] was Servant Jones. This first Servant Jones in our study is mentioned in his father's will of 1727[44] as a child and therefore would have been b. between 1707 and 1727. His earliest appearance in the existing Warwick Co. Court Records (2 Mar 1748) on a jury (/289) suggests that he would have been b. 1727 or before, agreeable to that calculated time frame.

Servant was foreman on Grand Juries in 1756 (/428) & 1760 (/498) inspector at Denbeigh Warehouse 4 Jun 1761. In 1759 an Ensign and 6 Aug 1761 Lt. Col. of the 1st company of militia (/527), and in the same year recommended to the Commission of Peace.

---

[43] Though Dr. Barry Hayes opines that the 3 daus of Matthew II were by his 1st wife, **Frances Servant [George]** and that the reference in the w. of brother Thomas Day was to the 1 ch of Eliz. [in *7JHA (Winter 2001), 1 /4*]. (footnote #s 39-42 not in use)
[44] The will is in *Isle of Wight Co. Will bk 3*.

17

This Servant Jones made his w. 20 Nov 1772, proved on 11 Feb 1773 in Warwick Co.[45] It names chen **Allen, Mary, Matthew, William, James Servant, John**, and grdau **Frances Servant**, dau of his deceased son **Phillip** And he mentions a brother **Albridgton**. A clause says:

> ...' By my deceased father's last Will and Testament the Reversion of several tracts or parcels of land will be my property at the death of my brother, Albridgton Jones, and when that shall happen my Will and desire is that my Executor shall bring suit against the person and all persons that shall have possession or claim the said lands, and if the said lands shall be recovered or any part thereof ...'

According to the rule of primogeniture, which would continue until 1787 in VA, Servant Jones could claim the right of reversion and argue that the lands 'given' in his father's will were actually lifetime grants and not permanent property rights.

Matt II married (2) **Elizabeth Day Ridley**, widow of **Nathaniel Ridley** who had died in 1719.[46] **Matthew Jones II** died testate in 1727/8. **Eliz.** was his ex until she d. in 1749, when their son '**Britton**' became ex of his fa's estate. After 1712 **Matt II** seems to have been largely involved in Isle of Wight County. He was not called 'Jr.' in documents near or at the time of his death, but may have used that suffix in Warwick County during the life of his father.

Nathaniel Ridley   First let's look at the descendancy from **Nath'l Ridley** (c1680-1719); he lived in IoW Co. and d. there 1718/19.[49] He m. **Elizabeth Day** (c1685-1749) in 1706. Their chen were **Lydia** who m. **George Portlock, Elizabeth Ridley** who m. **Jesse Browne, Jas** who m. **Jane Smith, Thos., Nath'l [II]** who m. **Prisc. Applewhaite**, and **Mary Ridley** who m. **Francis Jones** nephew of her sister by her 2nd m. (allowing us to believe that **Mary** was only a baby when her fa d.); McS says they moved to NC where he wrote his w. in 1750.

The d. of **Elizabeth Day's** brother ,**Thomas Day**, was 19 Jan 1723 in I of W Co. and recorded 24 Feb 1723 [*Great Bk. trns. /90*. MJ was ex.] The w.

---

[45] Servant's w. is in Dunn:2019/19. An ex was Robert Lucas.
[46] The will of **Nathaniel Ridley** was recorded 27 Jul 1719 in *Isle of Wight County*. *(footnotes 47-48 not in use)*
[49] *Great Book trns./79;orig. p.1*

of **Thos. Day** mentions 'sister Jones' and 'bro-in-law **MJ**.' *VA Land, M., & Pr .Recs, 1639-1850.*

It appears that Matthew Jones II became a Justice of Warwick County beginning in 1713 (/203); his age at that time would have had to be 21 or more, which would place his date of birth at 1692 or before. Probably his b. year was actually c1675-8 (see later calculations). Not only his father lived in Warwick County and was a justice there, but also the same is true of Matthew II himself for part of his adult life. On 13 Oct 1727 (i.e. before Matthew II's w.), the recording of a land deed notes ' Matthew Jones Gent., [Matthew II] 380 acres in Isle of Wight County, N side of Nottoway R., beginning near the Main Rd. going to Dr. Browns' [Nugent,... III/339].

On 12 May 1747 (20 years aft the d. of **Matthew II!**) Matt's exec. and widow **Elizabeth** sold 200 acres from Matt's estate to **Thos. Binns** of Surry Co. The sale was in Brunswick Co., VA.[50] Witnesses were **Albridgton Jones, Harwood Jones, Servant Jones** ('of Warwick Co.'), **Thos Brantley,** and **William Richards. Marget Jones** had m. **Thos Binns,** bef. 2 Oct 1744. There was a m. **John Jones**. to **Eliz. Binns** in Sussex Co. in 1758,[51] and there was a Binns Jones. in the same co.[52]—presumably a son of John and Eliz – who m. **Eliz Cargill in 1781.**

Records of 6 Sep 1750[53] indicate a resettlement of Matthew II's estate, no doubt occasioned by the d. of his widow, **Elizabeth**, distributing sums to several persons incl chen of **Nat'l Ridley** (or their husbands) and of **Matthew Jones II** showing also that **Matt's** daus were m. (The actual years of their ms. was likely in the 1740s).

To shed light on the Isle of Wight County activities of the Matthew whom I dub **Matthew [II]**, **Ridgell's** [54] unpublished report (his p.22) says:

> Matthew Jones [II] was a member of the vestry of the Old Brick Church [later known as St. Luke's] in Isle of Wight County and was first listed as a member of the Vestry in the Upper Parish [Newport Parish], which met 5 Jun 1724. In several of the records he is listed as **Captain Matthew Jones.**

---

[50] *Brunswick Co. Deed Bk 3 pp 350 & 360*
[51] *Sussex Co. M. Index #7*
[52] *Sussex Co. M. Index #9*
[53] *I of W Co. WB 5 /322*
[54] Unpublished [1970?] report on the MJH in the Historian's Office at Fort Eustis, VA, found c1989-91.

Chain of Wills   We are most fortunate to have an unbroken series of w. recs from 1727 to 1824 for one segment of this family, namely the succession **Matthew II** (1727), **Servant Jones** (thanks to Lyndon Hart of LVA for supplying this) of 1772-3, **Allen** (of Bourbon) of 1784, and **Wm** of 1824. All of them were in or related to Warwick Co.   **Matthew II** was the son of **Matthew I** (for whom no w. exists), **Servant** was the son of **Matthew II**, **Allen** a son of **Servant**, and **William** a son of **Allen**.

> **The W. of Matthew II** [*IoW Co. WB 3*]:   Item. I Give to my son **Servant Jones** my Tract of Land in Warwick County left to me by my father and Likewise I give him the following negros (Vizt) Sam, Vasco, Pegg, Ciss and likewise I Give the third part of the Cattle hogs sheep of the aforesaid plantation this being in full of his part or parsell of my Estate and I desire that my Sister **Marget Jones** and **My Cozen**[55] **Matthew** Jones to take the child and bring him up in the Fear of God out of the profits of the Estate
>
> .Item. I Give to my Daughter **Ann** my plantation I bought of Thomas **Briant** at Nottaway Swamp and if she dies without heirs then I give it to my Daughter Marget and these following negros (Vizt) Fillis, Frank. [She married **Thomas Holt** [Isle of Wight Will Book #6)].
>
> Item. I Give to my Daughter **Agethy** my Tract of Land which is in the Survey of **Henry Sommerlings** on Nottaway [River] to her and her heirs & for want of such heirs to my son **Albridgton** & likewise I Give her these following negros (Vizt) Frank, man Negro, Girl Lisa. [from Great Book transcription: 'Reversion of bequest to son **Albridgton**'].
>
> Item. I Give to my Daughter Marget all the Land that lyes on the road on East side of **Dr. Browns** including the Land in Applewhaite Neck and Chinkapen Neck and her heirs and for want of such heirs to my Daughter **Agethy** and I Give my Daughter **Marget** these following negros (Vizt) Peg, Roger, Nance. [**Marget** m. **Thos Binnns**   (*IoW Deed Book #6)*].

---

[55] 'Sister' and 'Cousin' often had general meanings. A specific example of 'cousin' meaning 'nephew' is in Shakespeare's *Much Ado About Nothing* in which Leonardo says to his brother (his real brother) 'How now, brother, where is my cousin, your son' [Act I, Scene 2]. Though that was earlier, Shakespearian English was similar to the English of the VA colony.   Possibly he had both a sister and the daughter named Marget, but no record shows the former.

Item. I Give to my son **Britten** one Tract of Land Containing one hundred and forty four acres in Warwick County that I bought of **Edward Kippin** and all the Land at Nottaway River that I have not bequeathed before I Give to him likewise and likewise I Give to my son **Britten** these following negros (Vizt) Frank Fillis at Nottaway and Charity.

Item. I Give to my loving wife the following negros Tomboy, Will, Jenny, Sarah; my will and desire is that my wife may dispose of these negros among her Children as she thinks fitt.

Item. I desire that my Land and Stock in Brunswick County may be sould & the proceeds of it to return to my Estate and it is my Desire that when all my debts and Legacies are paid I leave the rest and remainder of my estate to be equally divided between my loving wife, **Britton, Ann, Marget, Agethy**, my children wherefore I appoint and leave my wife fully and soly Executrix of this my last will and Testamt. and making all other wills by me made [void] as witness my Hand & seal this 28 Jan 1727/8.

This w. lists the daus **Ann, Agethy, and Marget**. We note that the daus of the grfa **Francis Albridgton** also included besides **Elizabeth, Anne and Margaret**. Matt II's son Britten ('**Britton**' elsewhere in the will) m. (1) **Eliz. Simmons** bef. 5 Jun 1746, (2) Mrs. Mary **Wilson**, widow, bef. 1750; and 3) Mrs. **Mary Simmons**, widow, on 19 Feb 1770. '**Britton**' (**Albridgton**) made his will 22 Sep 1784; in the codicil of 1785 he adds a bequest to **Ann Simmons**. **Servant Jones** made his w. 20 Nov 1772, proved on 11 Feb 1773 in Warwick Co.

Matt II designates '**Sister Marget**' and '**my Cozen Matthew Jones**' to take care of his (under age) son **Servant**. Doubtless 'cozen' means nephew, i.e. a son of one of his siblings. And he had a sister named **Marget**.

The first item in the will shows that he got a Warwick County tract from his father. He (**Matt II**) gave this tract to his son **Servant Jones**. By calculation Servant would have been born c1713-1717, so he would have been c11-14 years old at his father's death. (See '**Servant**' section.) It is unknown what disposition was made of the remaining cattle after the bequest of Item I; by law his wife would probably be entitled to one-third, but that still leaves another third to be accounted for.

The mini-chart of the line from **Matthew II** *is:*

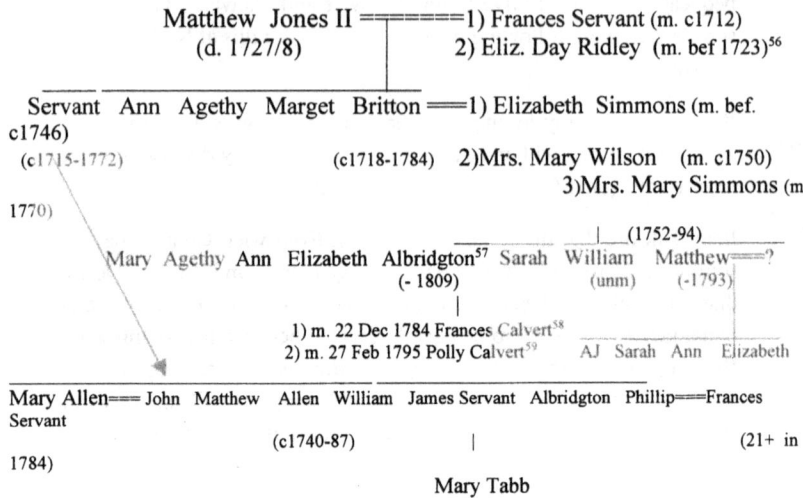

Ann Jones had m. **Thomas Holt**, and **Marget Jones** m. **Thomas Binns**. Both, with their husbands, conveyed to their brother **Albridgton Jones** *on 2 Oct 1744 the property in So'ton Co., VA adjoining* the Main Rd. and **Dr. Browne**. In a 2nd deed on the same day, they conveyed to **Albridgton** the Nottoway land patented by **Matthew** II bef. he made his w. in 1727.[60] **Agethy** m. **Thos. Harvey, Mary** m. **Ben Jarrell, Sarah** m. **Rev. Hen. Burges**, the later **Ann** (dau of **AJ**) m. **Gen. Lawrence Baker, Eliz.** m. (1) **Col. Miles Harvey**, (2) **Benjamin Baker**.[61]

For the decendancy from **Matthew II** and **Frances Servant** researchers might also consult 2 other sources: the Lee and Wills family Bibles. *6T146-7* for the Wills Bible and **Mrs. Donald C. Adams** for the Lee Bible.

[1773 Servant Jones' will:]   In the Name of God Amen I **Servant Jones** of the Parish & County of Warwick gent[n] being sick & weak of body but of perfect

---

[56] *IoW002*
[57] *So'hampton Co. WB4 /566*
[58] *In Southampton Co. VA [VA Compiled Marriages, 1660-1800]*
[59] *At Southampton Co., VA; in Chapman, [Isle of Wight Marriages 1748-1800]* and *VA., M. Records.*
[60] From article by Dr. Hayes in *7JHA2* (Spring 2001) /2 citing Chapman, *Ws. of So\hampton Co.* /503
[61] McS /235 citing Chapman & Knorr *Marriages* ...pp 28, 29, & 32

Mind and Memory knowing all Men must die Do commit my Soul to the Almighty God in shure & certain Hope of everlasting Life through the meritorious Suffering of my Blessed Saviour Jesus Christ my body to be decently buried at the Discretion of my Executors hereafter named and so hereby authorize them to execute this my last Will and Testament revoking all others made by me whatsoever   Item I give and devise unto my Son **Allen Jones** the Land I now live on to him and his Heirs forever likewise I give my said Son Allen my grey Mare to him and his Heirs   Item my Will and Desire is that all my Slaves and their Increase with the Stocks and other Personal Estate to be sold at publick Sale at twelve Months Creditt the Purchasers giving Bond and approved Security to my s^d Executor and the Money arising therefrom to be equally divided amongst my six children **Matthew , Mary, William, James Servant, John,** and my Grand Daughter **Francis Servant** (Daughter of my deceased Son **Phillip Jones**) and in Case my Grand Daughter dies under age or without lawful Issue then her Part to be equally divided between my two Sons **James Servant** and **John.**   Item by my deceased Fathers last Will and Testament the Reversion of several Tracts or Parcell of Lands will be my Property at the Death of my Brother **Albridgton Jones** and when that shall happen my Will and desire is that my Exor shall bring Suit against the Person and all Persons that shall have Possession or Claim the said Lands and if the said Lands shall be recovered or any Part thereof that then my Will is that the Lands so recovered shall be sold to the highest Bidder at twelve Months Creditt the Purchasers to give Bond and approved Security to my Exor and the Money therefrom arising to be equally divided amongst my Children **Allen, Matthew Mary Albridgton, William , James , John** and Grand Daughter **Francis Servant**   Item I do hereby appoint my Son **Allen** Guardian to my son **John** to educate and bring him up as he shall think proper. I do hereby appoint my Son Allen Jones and **Robert . Lucas** Exors of this my last Will & Testament bearing date the 20th Day November 1772   **Servant Jones** [seal]   Signed Sealed and published in presence of **Francis Lee   Cuthbert Hubbard**

[reverse:] At a court held for Warwick County Feby 11th 1773 This Will was presented in Court by the Exors therein named who made Oath thereto according to Law and the same being proved by the Oaths of the Witnesses thereto is ordered to be recorded and on the Motion of the said Exors who entered into Bond with **William Wills** and **John Dowsing** their Securities in the Penalty of £2000 & Certificate is granted them for obtaining a Probat thereof in due Form

 a Copy   Teste   **Richd Cary** C.Cu_

The 1787 w. of **Allen Jones**[62] (c1749-1787), the 1st son of the 1st Servant **Jones**, shows: m. (1) **Mary Tabb** c1762,[63] (2) __?, and (3) **Lucy Moss** 18 Feb 1773.[64] The chen of these 3 ms. were (1) **Bourbon and Mary, (2) Allen** and **Nancy** and **(3) Lucy (1780-)** and **Serviento. Lucy** m. **Mathew Wills** c1780-1827) 29 Sep 1801, **Phillip**, son of Servant, had a dau, **Frances Servant Jones** (under age in 1784), and **John** m. **Mary Allen**; the unm. sons were **Matthew, James Servant,** and **Albridgton.**

Allen's w. also names brother **William**, thus showing connections to both generations. **Allen**'s w. says he had made deeds of gift to his eldest chen and that he later recorded them in the General Court in Warwick Co. 20 Oct 1787. He mentions buying land from his brother **William** – 'part of Maj. Jones estate.' **John Jones Sr.** (1779-) m. **Servant Sr. Sarah Hubbard** in 1803 and had several chen incl **Scervant Jones**. **John Jr's** sons incl William, Servant Jones [Sr.] and **Francis** M. (1806-). By **John Jr's** 2nd m.; the ch was **Henry Francis Jones**

[1824 Will of William Jones Sr: I **William Jones** sen^r do make and ordain this my last will and testament as follows: I give to my wife all my Interest in the Estate of **Carter Burwell** acquired in right of my marriage with her, also all the property I purchased at his Sale, which shall be in my possession at the time of my death upon her paying what money if any may be due from me to the said estate. Also four Oxen, Six Cows, and four Sows with their pigs or shoats, fifty barrels of Corn, a Sufficiency of fodder, Twenty five Bushels of wheat 1000^{lbs} Pork and One beef; also one feather Bed without furniture and my Carriage & Harness. This Bequest being expressly intended by me in full satisfaction

---

[62] The w. of Allen Jones was written in 1783 with a codicil in 1787. It was found in the Hustings Court, 1787-1795, for York Co., pp 1-3. There are 2 sets of pages 1-20. In examining this original book, it was necessary to turn the bk. upside down and read from the back. It was in York Co. recs even though he says that he is 'resident on Bourbon in the Parish and County of Warwick.' Allen owned at least 92 acres in York Co. [General Index to *deeds 1777-1956 /415],* d. there and met the rules by which he was legally deemed a resident of that co. (Yorktown was incorporated the same year [on 5 Mar 1787]). Witnesses were **Pate Wills** and **Seymour Powell**. Ex. was **William Goosley**.
[63] **Mary Tabb's** w. is at ECC 25 Dec 1783 [*6T146]*
[64] *York Co. Marriage Bonds.* And see *US Sons of the Amer. Rev. app.* (re descendancy from **Cpt. Thos Wills**) which gives her b. as 1778. the d. as 1849, and the m. as 1803. A lineage bk. re that descendancy from Thos. Wills gives the dates of **Lucy Jones'** spouse, **Matthew Wills**, as 1775-1827, and after them **William Gilliam** (1801-80) m. **Lucy Servant Wills** in 1828.

of Dower in my Estate. I give to my son **William Jones [Jr]** my Brick House plantation, Queen Hive and half of Green Swamp to him and his heirs forever.

I give my White House plantation, and the other half of Green Swamp to son **Francis Jones** and his heirs forever. Notwithstanding the last mentioned Bequests to my Two Sons **William** and **Francis**, it is my wish in the event of the death of either under age and without issue, that the Same as given to such son so dying as aforesaid Should go To my Son **Hinde** to him and his heirs forever

I give to my Son **John Jones** my slaves Fanny, Julius, Bob, William and Lucinda To him and his heirs forever, but in case my said Son Should die under age and without issue, and I leave another child by my wife whether it be a son or Daughter, I give the said Slaves to Such child and its heirs forever.

I give to **Elizabeth Ann Upshaw Yates**[65], the Daughter of my first Wife twenty dollars and in the event of the death of either of my children, it is expressly my will and desire, that She Shall not come in for any other or greater share or proportion of my Estate than the said sum of twenty dollars.

The balance of my estate and property of every kind after the payment of my just debts, I give and bequeath to my two remaining children **Mary** and **Hinde,** and should the payment of my debts so exhaust my estate hereby intended for Mary and Hinde as that their respective shares shall not amount in value to twelve hundred dollars each, then and in that case, it is my Will and I do direct that my sons **William** and **Francis** in consideration of the land given them, pay equally a Sum Sufficient to make Such Share or proportion Twelve Hundred dollars To my said children Mary and Hinde. It is further my will, that my said daughter Shall have my mahogane ... Bedstead, bed curtains belonging thereto, and furniture including the white counterpane formerly her Mother's and also the Bed quilt given to her by her Grand Mother.   I appoint my friend **Scervant Jones** and my son **William** my Executors, to whom I give full power to Sell if necessary any part of my personal estate for the purpose of purchasing, or in other way to arrange or secure the Swan Tavern made over to me by Mr **Wills** or to obtain the debt or money thereby Secured and in the event of their purchasing said property, it is my wish that it shall be by them sold again and the money arising from such sale or the property itself in their discretion as the same must be acquired out of Mary and Hinde's share of my Estate, is to be equally divided between them.

---

[65] Wilkerson,... 129 shows **Eliz (Upshaw) Jones** m. 1809 to **Thos. Harwood.**

I hereby revoke all former wills and Testaments by me made confirming and ratifying this as my only true last will and Testament. In Witness whereof I have hereunto set my hand and affixed my seal this 13th day of June 1824.   **William Jones [Sr]**   [seal] Signed and sealed as the will and Testament of said William   Jones sen^r in our presence **Edm^d Waller, Sarah C Allen**   At a court held for Warwick County this 9th day of December 1824 this Will was proved by the oaths of **Edmund Waller and Sarah C Jones** late Sarah C Allen the witnesses thereto. Sworn to by **Scervant Jones** one of the executors therein named and ordered to be recorded and certificate for obtaining a probat thereof in due form was granted the said executors

A significant feature in this succession of wills is the chain of ownership of the MJH. **Matthew II**, gave the property to his eldest son, **Servant**. Then Servant passed it on through his sons to **William S.**, who gave it to his son, **William S. [Jr]**. **William Jr.** then sold 'the brick house' (It was then over a century old) at auction on 20 May 1832 in order to pay certain debts and thereby to prevent his bro **Francis M.** (security) from any liability in that regard, The buyer **Bennet Wood**, paid $1,180 for the parcel (250 acres) [Dunn: 2018 /364]. How it got back into Jones ownership is not known, but **Henry Francis Jones** was born there in 1839, so that means that his parents lived there also at that time – possibly as renters from Mr. Wood.

A **MJ** b. 1768 in NC m. (1) **Sarah Kimbrough** 31 Jan 1797.[66] The b. years of their chen ranged from 1797 to Jun 1808. Wife **Sarah** d. 16 Dec 1808. MJ m. (2) Eliz __ 1 Feb 1810. MJ d. in 1843. [*NC Digital Collections, Family Recs*]. As this info reportedly came from a family Bible of **Nathaniel K Jones** (1800-1882), it's possible that the **MJ** mentioned was a son of that NJ. This NJ reportedly m. **Caroline Jones** and **Lucy Ann Norment**.

York Judgments & Orders, #3 1759-63/438 w. pr.15 Nov 1762 Mary, wife?

***

Allen Jones

The name occurs importantly in the foregoing will connections, and also appears at several times in various places, e.g. a Sr. and a Jr. in Chowan Co., NC (19th century). We also include **Bourbon Jones** here, as this name is closely associated with **Allen.**

---

[66] *Index to 1800 fedcen*

NC Estate Files record the d. intestate of an **Allen Jones** on 22 Jan 1820 (whose orphans were **Elizabeth, Margaret Jones** and **Edmund Jones [Jr.]**). A **William Jones** was appt'd adm. of the estate of this Allen Jones. Allen was the son of **Edmund Jones [Sr.]**; **William Jones** was a legatee of the same Edmund, the elder. Allen attended William & Mary College in Williamsburg. 'Our' Allens are not to be confused with Brigadier General **Allen Jones of NC**.

Misc An Allen Jones' w. dated 21 Sep 1824 [*6T47*] names bros **William, Henly, Daniel, Wm M**. ex (bro)

6T47 **Henly T. Sr**, nephew of **William M.**;   dau of **Hen.: Mrs. Hunter Wheeler,** Her dau: **Mary Allen Jones, Henly T. Jr**. wife: **Mary Southall**, dau of **Albert G. Southall**

Another source (*8H, Chap. XIII/34-5*) shows a land trsfr from William Cary to **Allen Jones** on 26 Aug 1711 for £720.

Intriguing records in the VA Cos. of Granville and Sussex, and in *The Southside Virginian* 2/1/16-20 and 12/1/25-27, indicate that there were Allen and other Jones connections related to the **Binns, Masons** & other families there--but without sufficient info for us. We *do* know of the two Jones/Binns ms. already cited but we do not know, for example, the parentage of **Lucy Binns Jones** (1817-1882). A future researcher might find records to make all of this clear.

Halifax Also in NC was a bond by Allen Jones, **Willie Jones & Harwood Jones** of Apr 1768. The above bound Allen is appointed clerk of the Superior Court of Justice for the District of Halifax ...in the presence of __**Haynes** [and] **Edw Montfort.**

Wake Another Allen Jones' estate is noted in *NC Estate Files*: this one d. intestate 29 Sep 1851 in Wake Co. His wife was Sarah. This man was b. c1770, d. 21 Aug 1851 [*Henley*]. He could have served in the War of 1812 [*Muster Roll pp 324, 414, 758+ NC*].

NC Co. Ms. show a m. of Allen Jones 1 Jan 1821 to **Polly Jones** in Wake Co.

Warwick *1810 fedcen for War. Co.* **Allen Jones** 1 male under 10, one 26-45; 1 fem.16-26   3 slaves

York *York Judgments & Orders, May 1763 – Aug 1765*   **MJ & Matthew Hubbard**   suit   18 Jul 1763

York *Judgments & Orders, #3 1759-63/225*   wit. 15 Mar 1761

6T48: Allen Jones of Yorktown   grantee 10 Oct 1783   cites York recs

York, Hustings Crt Allen Jones [Sr] 1787 codicil.   To enable ex to sell lnds bought at Savage Town

The adm. of an Allen Jones was sued in the *Chancery Recs of York Co.* by **William H. Jones**, infant, apparently for an action involving 31 slaves. The Index Number 1831-003==the year (1831) of the action. [*LVA, VA Memory, Chancery Recs Box 6*].

York Ms 1772-1849   Allen m. **Lucy Moss** 18 Feb 1773

York Deeds 6/301   Allen & Lucy grantors: Lot   Wmsbg 20 Feb 1786

York Deeds 6/415   Allen Jones (dec'd) grantor to **Francis Lee** 92 a. in Yorktown 21 Sep 1789

York Ws. 10, /1811, 511   w. 21 Sep 1824, rec. 16 Nov 1824

York, Hustings Crt Allen Jones   dfdt in suit; abated due to d. of dfdt. **John Moss** pltf

York Deeds grantor to **Sheldon Moss** lots in Wmsbg

York, Hustings Crt Allen Jones   orphs' suit 3 Nov 1789. **Mary, Bourbon Allen, Nancy.** **Sheldon Moss**, trustee; **William Goosley** ex.. suit for £514 fr est

York, Hustings Crt   Allen Jones   w. pr. 26 Nov 1787. Oaths: **FJ, Pate Wills, Seymour Powell**

York, Hustings Crt /33 **Bourbon Jones**   affidavit 24 Mar 1788 "With int. fr 13 Oct 1787 (prob date of d. of Allen)

York, Hustings Crt /12, 17   **Allen Jones** 34 Sep1787 in arrest; non-performance of debt   [qestionable-RD]

York, Hustings Crt /18 Allen Jones "late of Yorktown" inv: goods & *chattels at Bourbon*

York, Hustings Crt /16 Allen Jones est sale 22 Dec 1787 at Bourbon

York, Hustings Crt /16 Allen Jones Sr sale cont'd to 4 Jan. J. Grant for a coffin

York Judgments & Orders, #3 1759-3/225 chancery 16 Aug 1762

York Order Bk 4, 1774-84/12 Allen Jones 21 Mar 1774 suit

York Order Bk 1795-1803 **Ann Jones**, orph of Allen? **Sheldon Moss** apptd gdn 18 Apr 1796.

York Order Bk 1795-1803/108 **Servient**, orph of Allen, JJ apptd gdn 18 Apr 1796.

York Order Bk 1795-1803/108 **Servient**, orph of Allen, JJ apptd gdn 18 Jul 1796. Sec: **John & Bourbon**

York Order Bk /423 JJ's gdn acct for his wards c1800

York Order Bk 12/227, 1829-1835 **Henley Jones** orph of Allen Jones c1832

York Jdmts & Ords 1768-70/84 Allen Jones 15 Aug 1768 suit

***

Ships In addition to ocean-going vessels, existing early VA records indicate the operation of ferry service,[67] mentioning ferries operating across the James River to and from Mulberry Island. In some English duplicates of lost Virginia records, **Matthew Jones** is also listed as part owner in two ocean-going vessels: one is described as the Dispatch of Bristol, square stern, built in VA in 1696 with a capacity of 60 tons. The second, the Expectation of Bristol, a briganteen, built in James City [Jamestown] in 1698, had a capacity of 100 tons. That Matthews I & II were both merchants is apparently beyond dispute. *Cognets,*[68] lists ships entering Rapahanock River 11 Nov 1699 to 24 Jun 1700. **Matthew I** could have been involved with commerce between England and VA, and it is not surprising that a scribe would note down facts of *ownership* more readily than those of *residence*.

---

[67] (footnote not in use)
[68] *English Duplicates*

Matthew Jones [III] (-9 Nov 1744) was prob the jury foreman [/131] in 1729, the one who m. **Martha Harwood**, was a grandson of **Matthew I** (/514) and probably the son of **Francis II**. Assuming an age in 1729 of at least 21, he was born in 1708 or before. In 1729 he would unambiguously have been '**Matthew Jones of Warwick**.' He probably is the:'**Cozen Matthew** ' referred to in Matthew II's will. Though direct evidence is non-existent he can be eliminated as a child of **Albridgton Jones II** or **Matthew II**, for whom wills exist, and of **John II**, who seems very unlikely. That leaves the brothers **Nathaniel** and **Francis** – the latter seeming more probable (because of a son named **Francis Jr**. [Jr.= III] and the gift of land to him). **Francis III** made his w. 9 Nov 1744,[69] but we don't know if he d. soon after that or several years afterwards.

Matthew IV

Gr'grson of **MatthewI** (-1771): A Bible of the Chisman family shows[70] that **Mary Chisman** married **Harwood Jones**, son of ' **Matthew Jones** of Warwick' & **Martha**, his wife, 2 Oct 1744. Harwood Jones died 9 Feb 1771, and Mary [Chisman] died 12 Mar 1781.

MJ Related or unrelated

Misc.   Boddie, *Hist. VII/ 93* Matthew Jones II 1665-1736 [wrong-RD] m. **Martha Harwood**; son: **Francis Jones** of Warwick & Edgecombe.

Virkus, ...VII/471   MJ 1682 to IoW Co. then Mul. Is. [doubtful-RD]

MJ   militia   1754   VA   *Washington's paybill*

Lt. Col. **George** . **Washington's** VA troops in Fr & Ind War
Aug. Rec.2/49, *VMHB I/280, Wash Mss 11/111,*   and *Eckenrode/5*

MJ   militia   9 Jul 1754   /51,131,237,136 [procla. of 1754], 238 [6 Nov 1772]   *Bockstruck/46*

MJ   militia pvt 1754   August Co., **Cpt. Andrew Lewis'**
Com.   Tyler, *Men/116-7 & 119* (bounty money)

---

[69] According to the indenture of sale of the land willed to him [the indenture is in *IoW Co. DB 9* /92 and was dated 13 Nov 1752.]
[70] *York Co. Records 20 Jul 1778* (IV /167 & /174) and s.a. *13WM/1/70.*

MJ   Pvt militia   9 Jul 1754 VA   Com. of **Andrew Lewis**.
[Clark, *Colonial* /285 + 305]

US and Canada, Passenger ... MJ arrival in VA 1682

A **MJ** b. 1768 in NC m. (1) **Sarah Kimbrough** 31 Jan 1797.[71] The b. years of their chen ranged from 1797 to Jun 1808. Wife Sarah d. 16 Dec 1808. MJ m. (2) **Eliz** __ 1 Feb 1810. Matthew Jones d. in 1843. [*NC Digital Collections, Family Recs*]. As this info reportedly came from a family Bible of **Nathaniel K Jones** (1800-1882), it's possible that the MJ mentioned was a son of that NJ. This NJ reportedly m. **Caroline Jones** and **Lucy Ann Norment**.

Brunswick   **MJ** of I of W. Co. 7 Jul 1726   200 acs N.L. in Brunswick Co., S side of Maherin R.   Nugent, *Cavaliers and Pioneers* III/314 + 525?

Chatham Wheeler, *History of NC* [vol. I /86] shows **MJ** apptd major Apr 1776 in Chatham Co., NC   [34 mi W of Raleigh]. Chatham Co. & Guilford Co. formed from Orange 1770 "Thus finished the military org. of the State." and of Hillsboro, NC, but **MJ** representing Chatham Co. wi **Elisha Cain** 21 Aug 1775, and in the General Assembly in 1783. *DAR recs.* /498 show him, also in Hillsboro, as a delegate with Elisha Cain to the Provincial Congress 21 Aug 1775.

Min NC Senate v, 12/800   MJ apptd jp 12 Aug1774; He resigned 17 Aug 1776.

Edgecombe   Boddie, *Historical... VII/93*   **MJ II** 1665-1736 [?-RD] m. **Martha Harwood**. Son: **FJ** of War. & Edgecombe   [prob incorrect-RD]

Halifax Co., NC   Boddie, *Southside VA Fams* I/76-7 shows MJ as a witness on /7 & 42 slaves. Mar 1772 in Halifax Co., NC, adj **Nathaniel Bradford**, citing *Will Bk 12/362*.

IoW   An est. account of 29 Jun 1736 is shown for MJ in IoW *[Great Book /125]*. This name appears in the same source (p.121 [orig.49] dated 1734, and p. 198 [orig. 43] dated 1760), the latter is an est. acct and is divided into 4 parts. Obviously the est. accts indicate the ds. of 2 different people, who might or might not belong to this line –' **Matthew Jones'** not being a name

---

[71]*Index to 1800 fedcen*

exclusive to this line of inquiry— the following, however, brings the matter into consideration: *VA Land, M., & Pr. Recs, 1639-1850* shows a pr. for MJ 29 Jun 1736; cites Bk 4-21, and a w. for **MJ** 28 Mar 1757, pr.5 Jan 1758, naming fa **Abraham** and chen incl **MJ & JJ.**

Boddie *Historical.../79, 92-3* thinks MJ I is a desc. of **Ed Bennet** and b-in-law of **Thos. Day.**

Nugent... **MJ** land 13 Oct 1727

IoW Co, Wills show a will of 4 Oct 1782 recorded 29 Oct 1784.

Chapman, *IoW Ms.* /27, shows **MJ's** m. 1734 in I of W Co., VA, to __ William   And m. to **Elisa. Ridley** 1723

An inventory was returned in IoW Co. for **MJ** on 1 May 1760. [*VA, Land, M., & Pr. recs, 1639-1850,* citing bk 7-18].

A Matthew is listed as a son (wi son **Britain** et al) in the w. of **Samuel Jones** [*VA, Land M., and Probate Recs, 1639-1850,* and Great Book trns./225 {orig. 74}].

IoW Deeds 100 a. in IoW Co. to **MJ** from **George Portis 1744**

MJ 1 May 1760   inv returned [to court] by **Abraham Jones** [Chapman, *IoW Ws 04/18]*

VA, IoW Co. Recs, 1634-1951 – Deed Recs 1784: **Britan Ward** sells land in IoW Co. to **MJ**

VA Land, M., & Pr. Recs, 1639-1850 **MJ Jr** vital: 5 Mar1713, civil: 25 Mar 1713 IofW

VA, IoW Co. Recs, 1634-1951 –   **MJ** apprsl of **Peter Deberry** 27 Apr 1713

VA, IoW Co. Recs, 1634-1951 – Deed Recs 1760: deed, MJ of York Co., grantor, sells to **Jas Watson** of the co. of IoW 250 a. in IoW which formerly belonged to MJ the elder and by him given to his 2 boys MJ & FJ...[FJ sold his part 13 Nov 1752 to MJ, Jr (p. 17)]

MJ of I of W. Co. 7 Jul 1726   200 acs N.L. in Brunswick Co., S side of Maherin R   Nugent, *Cavaliers*...III/314 + 525?

VA Land, M., & Pr.Recs, 1639-1850 w. of **John Asque** 5 Mar 1713 pr. 25 May 1713

Meck.   Bockstruck /137   a MJ   1774 in Dunsmore's War

Nansemond   1790 feden p.33, for Nansemond

So'ton   Schreiner-Yantis, *1787 census*   MJ   (Southampton Co)

W Bk I South'n Co., VA /102   **MJ** Inv. & Appr.14 Dec 1752
Elizabeth   ex. dec'd

Col. Britton Jones   1813   Southampton Co., VA
Polly Calvert, wife; MJ, father   6T276

Wulfeck I/ 4 /58   MJ m. – **Tignall.**   cites *11 Tyler 33*

RegMaSth /635 MJ m. 20 Jan 1785   Southampton Co., VA
Molly Crumpler.   s.a. Hart & Nichol/568 top

The 1787 tax lists for that co. [So'ton] identify 2 **MJ**s in Nottoway Parish; notations in the margin show one at Black Creek ("B Creek") and one at Nottoway Swamp ("Nott"). These areas were the portion of So'ton Co. between the Nottoway and Blackwater Rivers. The area had been settled as early as 1700-1710. The Black Creek neighborhood was in the N half while Nottoway Swamp was some 7 miles SW on a tributary of the Nottoway River. ... 'Matt Nott' ... named a son AJ and he transferred to him 1132 a. Another & and more wealthy **Albridgton, Col. AJ, Sr.** ... was taxed for 1689 a. in 1795. **Matthew 'B Creek'** was credited with only 150 a. in 1795, "therefore of a different socio-economic class." He descended from 3 generations of **Thomas Joneses.** ... In 1782 Thos. (IV) willed 150 a. to his son Matthew and another 150 a. to his dau, **Sarah Johnson.**' [This Matthew was apparently not a descendant of Matthew I, but might confuse.]

Surry   *VMHB /XIX/56* MJ w. 17 Feb 1773   Surrey Co.

Sussex   *Sussex Co. Wills* C 27-8   MJ inv 17 Feb 1773

Wake   Haun, *Wake* ... shows several acquisitions of land 1779-1807:
119/409/#72   **MJ Sr.** land 11 Oct 1800. Little Cr, S side; 100 acs adj lines of MJ.   9/281/#900 land 2 Jan 1779 both sides of Little Cr,
86/299/#983 land 1 Feb 1779 both sides Hurricane Br,. Enters 200 acs adj his own line & co. line.   105/372/#32   adj his own line.
123/416/#113 land 4 Oct 1801, Eloby's Cr. Enters 15 acs adj line of **Nathaniel Jones** 139/449/#309 land + water 30 Apr 1807 Neuse R; 5 acs of land and the water in the river

Wake Co. Deeds are at the Fam. Hist. Lib. in SLC on film 0238281.

Wake Co. M. Bonds: **MJ** to **Sally Kimbrough** 30 Jan 1797

1790 fedcen pp 87, 49 for Hillsborough Dist shows **MJ** in a household of 3 wh. males and 3 wh. fem. The same fedcen shows a **TJ** pp 88 & 104.

1800 fedcen MJ (742)

NC, Wake Co. Land Recs #366 (p. 248-9) granted to MJ 3498 a. in 'Western Dist.'

NJ Sr. (WP). grchen:**A,Ben Wooten** . W. pr. Feb 1810. Sons: **Nath'l m. Annah, Albridgton, Henry m.Peg Kimbrough**; wife **Anna B**. Daus - **Barbee, Polly Paxton**; bro **Matthew Jones**

Warwick Nugent, *Cavaliers* ... 118 + 45 **MJ** 29 Oct 1696 Warwick Co. Fisher's Creek. /316 MJ 25 Apr 1701 Warwick Co in re land of neighbor **Matthew Goodwin**

Dunn*: 2008/297*, citing *War. Co. Crt. Recs.* **MJ II** (d. In IoW) est apprsl returnd 6 Jul 1749

13W/70 **HJ** m. 2 Oct 1744 **Mary**, dau o **John Chisman** & wife **Eleanor Chisman**. HJ's prnts: **MJ & Martha**. Cites Chisman Bible

7T135 **John Jones Sr. of War.Co.** j.p. m. **Sarah Hubbard**, dau of **James Hubbard** and **Eliz Filmer.** Chen of JJ & Sarah: **John Jones Jr, Scervant, Sarah Hubbard Jones.** She (**Sarah Sr.**) bu .at St. Pauls in Norfolk; she m. (1) _Lucas, (2) **John Green.** JJ Jr son of JJ Sr & Mary [!], m. 1803 **Sarah Duncan**; sons: **William Scervant** (b. 3 Oct 1804), **Francis M.** (b. 1806). **William Scervant**, son of JJ Jr, m. (1) **Mrs. Sarah Carpenter Allen**, dau of **Benj. Watkins**, (2) **MaryAnn Wood**. William S. was fa of **William Benj. Jones ('Helllcat Billy'** (1828-1878) by Ms. Allen.

Dunn*: 2008/297*, citing *War. Co. Crt. Recs.* **MJ II** (d. In IoW) est apprsl returnd 6 Jul 1749

Wulfeck I 4 58 **MJ** d. 1772 'MJ of War.' cites *9T137*, 281; *11T33*

Ridgell/21 describes Matthew Jones **II** of Mul. Isle as b. ~~1665 and d. 1736~~ and husb. of **Martha Harwood**, dau of **Maj. Humphrey Harwood**. And says in 1728 he owned 10 tracts of land in IoW, Nottoway, Brunsw., and

War. Cos. inclu 2 houses and 2 tracts known as plantations in War. & on Nott. R.

Wulfeck , *Ms* ... I/ 4/58 **MJ [I]** b. c1640. Cites *11 T 33,* Boddie *17th/283.*

Hutton,... 142   c1600-1682   MJ burgess   wife: **Eliz.**

Hist. Off. at Ft. Eustis   Record: **Estelle (Webb) Powell** of Richmond from a meeting wi **Carl Cannon** c Oct '84 ... 'when **Rev Webb** d., the onion crop was $1 mil.'

Ridgell/142   **Randall Crew** [ex. for chen of Matthew I] was a burgess 1645-48 for Warwick Co. He cites Elliot, *Early Wills*, index to v. I, and II/179.

Another **MJ (Sr.),** not **Matthew I,** lived in War. Co., d. aft 1741, was the son of **FJ Sr.**, and had 2 sons, **FJ & MJ,** who were over 21 in 1752. MJ Sr. lived in War. Co., the son, FJ lived in War. Co; the other son, MJ, lived in IoW Co.   MJ Sr of War. Co. had purchased on 22 Mar 1741 land from **Mr. Portis** which he (MJ) bequeathed to his 2 sons. Then, on 13 Nov 1752, FJ sold his share to his bro. [See McS/184-7 and *VA, IoW Co. Recs,1634-1951.*] Another [uncorroborated-RD] acct of this is said to be in *IoW deeds 5 Jun 1760* 're 250 ac. from MJ & Mary, his wife, of York Co. to **Jas Watson,**[72] which anciently belonged to Matthew Jones the Elder and was given to his sons **MJ & FJ,** ... FJ sold his part to MJ; this MJ lived in York Co. where his w. of 10 Aug 1762[73] was proved 15 Nov 1762. It is too mutilated but mentions MJ and directs that a house be built for his wife in Martin's Hundred'.

VA COUNTIES (SWEM LIB.)   **Jones, Matthew** to list tythbls 21 May 1701 in the lower pct, Mulb. Is., Warwick Co., VA.

York   *VA, IoW Co. Recs, 1634-1951* – Deed Recs 1760: deed, MJ of York Co. , grantor, sells to Jas Watson of the co. of IoW 250 a. in IoW which formerly belonged to MJ the elder and by him given to his 2 boys **MJ & FJ**...[FJ sold his part 13 Nov 1752 to MJ, Jr (p. 17)].
York 7, 1684-87/316   MJ   suit 4 May 1687

---

[72] There is a ref. to Jas Watson in Boddie, *17th* to land of 1655 and see the **Watson** w. in *IoW BK A.*
[73] See *12W143*

York, Watkins' *transcription of Deeds, Orders, Ws #3,1657-1662/164:* Mr. **Jones** Middle Plantation tobacco 26 Mar 1661.

grantor 16 Jun 1818 *York Co.* to **Matt. Wills** "Lt.[lot] Yorktown"

York #3 Judgs & Ord 1759-1763 /438 MJ w. pr. 15 Nov 1762 York Co., VA by oaths of **John Wagstaff & Becky Harvey**; **Mary**: wife

York Ws, Invs 1760-1771 #21117 MJ of Yorkhampton Par. W. rec. 15 Nov 1762 York Co, VA dated 10 Aug 1762 . Wife: **Mary** "under age"; **Matthew**, son; bro **Francis**. *York [6T45]* Partly obliterated.

York#3 1759-63 /438 MJ w. proved 15 Nov 1762

MJ Yorkhampton Par., York Co. deed 5 Jun 1760 Isle of Wight Co., VA Mary wife. his bro was Francis

York Jdmts & Ords 1768-70 /43, 124, 201 20 Jun 1768

Wulfeck , *Ms* ... I /4 /58 MJ m. **Mary Lee**; his prnts: **Matthew Jones & Martha Harwood** res. York Co.; , cites *11 T 33*

9Tyler /137 MJ w. dated 10 Aug 1762 York Co., Pr. 15 Nov 1762. Wife: Mary [*Ridgell/197]:* dau of **John Tignall**. 'He moved to York Co.'

York Co. Ws & Admins, 1533-1811/117-8 MJ w. pr. 15 Nov 1762; p. 122-24, inv & appsl 17 Jan 1763

York Judgments & Orders, May 1763 – Aug 1765 MJ - **Matthew Hubbard** suit 18 Jul 1763

York #3 Jdmts & Ords 1759-63. w. pr. 15 Nov 1762. Oaths **John Wagstaff, Becky Harvey.** Wife: **Mary**

York #3 Jdmts & Ords 1759-63/455. MJ dec'd *inv. order 17 Jan 1763*

York Judgments & Orders, #3 1759-63/438 w. pr.*15 Nov 1762 Mary, wife?*

The Tingnall Family

This family has a strong bearing on the Matthew Jones lines. We assume that **Thomas Tingnall** is the father of **John Tingnall**, but the lack of records makes a certain determination impossible. A court record shows **John Tingnall** as 'orphan since 1655' (/544). On May 10, 1647, **Thomas Tingnall** was appointed Churchwarden of Nutmeg Quarter Parish in

Warwick County (/20), in the following month he was named administrator for an estate (*VA Genealogist* I pps 57 & 62), and surviving *Warwick County Court Orders, 1646-7* (pp 20, 596) show **Thomas Tingnall** as Church Warden and later defendant in a civil matter.[74] **John Tingnall** served as justice for Warwick Co. along with **Matthew Jones I** and later Matthew's son **Francis** during at least 1699-1702.[75] Francis evidently married a daughter of John Tingnall. Many descendants of Matthew I in the line of Francis Jones have the name 'Tingnall' (or 'Tignal'). John Tingnall had married Judith. In the quitrent rolls of 1713 **Judith Tingnall** was charged as the landowner of the 392 acres that her husb John had acquired earlier in Warwick County This entry is an indication that John had died before 1713; Nugent (op. cit.) p. 16 gives the acquisition date of the prop as 2 Nov 1705.

John also had land in Eliz City County (see Nugent), and an entry in that county's *Orders 1692-1705* /130[76] indicates that he took up an apprentice 18 Mar 1698, that he was probably a tailor and his wife a seamstress.

Jno Tingnall was an orphan in 1657? since 1655 (/544).

Francis II, (c1670-c1716), the first son

In dealing with the birth order of the chen of **Matthew [I] Jones** and **Elizabeth Albridgton** we place Francis first; several factors support the belief that Francis was the first-born son: 1) The naming pattern common at that time, says that the first-born son should be named after the *paternal grandfather*.[84] 2) In 1704 he was the only son appearing on the quitrent

---

[74] Another '**Mr. Tignall**' was listed as accountable for seven tithables (males over 16) a little later (1654) in Lancaster County, VA [*VMBH* /159]. This person might well have been related to **Thomas**, but in later years we will encounter others -- a fact which suggests that only one branch of the family settled in or near Warwick County.

[75] Concerning the Tingnall family it may be noted that a record (Gill, *Apprentices of VA 1623-1800* [at 'Ancestry' of Family History Library of LDS Church in SLC]) shows an apprentice seamstress to '**John & Judith Tignell**' in 1698 in Elizabeth City County (adjoining Warwick County on the east). Despite the spelling, this might be the Tingnall who served with Matthew I.

[76] Cited in Gill, *Apprentices of VA 1623-1800*, Salt Lake City, Ancestry. (footnotes 77-83 not in use)

[84] A Francis Jones died about 1669 when John Tingnall submitted an inventory of Jones' estate (no. 124/16/3). (VA Historical Society; a photocopy [per the author's records] is also in Rockefeller Library in Colonial Williamsburg, but was not found at the time of writing in either library). It is possible that this Francis Jones was the father of Matthew Jones I, thus also the paternal grandfather of this Francis Jones

rolls[85] (with 150 acres perhaps given him by his father)—suggesting that he was the beneficiary of the rule or custom of primogeniture. In 1704 a Francis Jones had 100 acres in Princess Anne County.[86] 3) Francis followed his father in public office [pps. 13, 66, 85, 90, 196 etc]. 4) He was sheriff over his brothers Nathaniel [12] and Albridgeton in 1714-1715 [/552][87]– which suggests that he was older and in a rather primary position among his siblings.

At Court   Francis is mentioned several times from 1699 to 1705 in the fragments of court records held by Swem Library[88] as an appraiser, plaintiff in a suit, and maker of a bond. If an age of 21 or more is assumed for him in 1699, he would have been born 1678 or before [but a calculation of the probable year of b. of Matthew II suggests the likelihood of c1670 or before for **Francis** a date that fits very well into the window of time during which the marriage of his parents **Matthew I** and **Elizabeth** took place. We can consider him '**Francis II**' (i.e. in the generation following that of his father, **Matthew [I] Jones**).

Francis [I] attains the office of sheriff in 1714 (and apparently through 1715) [/622]. It is likely that the later extant Warwick County Court Minutes (of 1748-1762) refer to another **Francis Jones;** there are many references there to a Francis Jones as Justice of the Peace, on the Commission of Peace, as a bondsman, etc., and ultimately sheriff.

Francis also served on the Warwick County Court with Matthew (presumably his father, Matthew [I]) in 1705 [/196] [1705 Orders at LVA]. He was on the court 1713-1714 (pp 599 & 607) --and perhaps also in the years for which records are not extant. Court records for 1705 listed **Francis Jones** as on the 'quorum' in 1714 (/647) (Cognets... / 29). He provided a security bond for **John Tingnall** in 1700 (/90) And in the same year he was appt'd sheriff (/622) (& McIlwaine III/371). The 1702 statement by **Miles Cary** recommending the appt of **Francis Jones** indicates that Francis was

---

, but unless or until the document is found, this particular item is uncertain.

[85] For the 1704 Quitrent rolls see Louis des Cognets, *English Duplicates of Lost Virginia Records* p. 187, and see *The Virginia Magazine of History and Biography Vol. 30, No. 4 (Oct., 1922)*, pp. 341-347, Published by: Virginia Historical Society.
[86] *VMBH* /345; There's no indication whether or not 'our' person is meant.
[87] And see McIlwaine, *Exec. Journals* ... III/371 & 398.
[88] Box 1, Folder 5 and Box 2, Folder 1. (*Order Book* Fragment) *1699-1701* [Their catalogue numbering as of the year 2000]). S.a. the *Orders 1705.*
He was appt'd sheriff for Warwick County 28 Apr 1714 & again in 1715 (confirmed by *LVA, Lost Records* that he was sheriff 5 May 1715).

c21 but not yet a justice, thus b. c1681 and in turn suggesting the m. year of his parents at c1680 or before.

Relationship with the Tingnalls

Francis [II] evidently married **Mary Tingnall**. Her father, **John Tingnall** was an associate of Matthew I, and he served with him on the court for at least the years 1699 (/68) to 1702 (/121) and he might have been close to the family for many more years (especially if the 1669 estate inventory actually pertained to the father of Matthew I). **John Tingnall** also owned land in Warwick County in 1704,[89] but we don't know the actual proximity to Jones' property. Warwick County Court records show him as an orphan there in 1655 (/544) (evidently the son of **Thomas Tingnall**, who had been a church warden for Nutmegquarter Parish in 1647. In 1701 John was appointed with other members of the court to list the titheables (so spelled) below Waters Creek (i.e, toward the southeastern end of the Island) while **Matthew Jones** also was appointed to the 'lower precincts of Mulberry Island Parish.'[90] (McSwain (her p. 173) mentions two other records[91] which refer to Matthew Jones's land in that region). In 1704 quit rent rolls, John Tingnall is shown with 392 acres in Warwick County. There is no mention of him after 1707 in the records. In 1713 the 392 acres are shown as belonging to 'Judeth Tignal' (Judith Tingnall).[92]

About the marriage: John Tingnall and **Matthew Jones I** were about the same age. They lived near each other, were both of the landed gentry class, and both served as magistrates of the County Court. Each had chen of marriageable age, a Miss Tingnall and a Mr. Jones. It isn't hard to believe that a marriage of these two actually took place, even without the evidence that emerges later. In any case most researchers believe Mary Tingnall to have m. FJ [II].

The chen of Francis [II] (c1670-c1715) & **Mary Tignall**   Although no existing records show the names of the chen of the family of Francis II and **Mary. Tingnall**, McSwain would attribute two chen to the family, namely **Matthew III** who m. **Martha Harwood** and **Francis III** who m. **Mary**

---

[89] McSwain, op, cit.
[90] For the Tingnall records see Dunn:2008 (3rd ed.) pps 20, 24, 53, 68, 71, 74, 75, 80-7, 90, 95, 99, 100-1, 104-5, 194, 544, 551, 583, 593.
[91] *Cavaliers and Pioneers* III/27 & 42
[92] Two quit rent rolls exist: for 1704 and 1713 for Warwick Co. The 1704 rolls are transcribed in *VMHB XXX* P. 345 and elsewhere; the rolls for 1713 are in the *Blathwayt Papers, Rockefeller Library, Colonial Williamsburg Foundation.*

Ridley (McS /183). This placement seems correct. She cites the *absence* of the Tignal name in all but the descendancy from Francis II, but *many* Tignals in the Francis II to **Matthew III** line to support the inclusion of Francis III & Matthew III in this family.

We would add another two chen to the **Francis Jones/Mary Tingnall** family: **Nathaniel** and **Britton** (Albridgton). This is based on the 1895 letters by Mrs. **Amelia Ann Whitaker**, in the vertical files in NC but copied in their entirety by Mrs. McSwain in her book. Though Mrs. Whitaker was then 79 and thus long removed in time from the immediate family of Francis Jones II, she was a *descendant* and deeply involved in her family history (as is shown by her letters (7 pages, single spaced, full of family history, [McS pp. 208-214]). Her info may be regarded as primary source material for matters close to her of which she has personal knowledge. Mrs. Whitaker says:

> 'I learned all I could about our family from my father and I had it traced out and written down, but it was lost with all my books and house and everything when the Yankees came. If I had saved that family tree it would give much information.' She adds that her father if he were still alive, would be 130 years old [i.e. b. c1764].

Notable in the work of Mrs. Whitaker is the inclusion of information not found in the works of either Camilla Davis or McSwain; this is especially true of the entire line down to Mrs. Whitaker's correspondent, **Susie Gentry**. There are disagreements between these works, and the next researcher must seek further records for clarification. In the absence of contrary contemporary documents, however, this information is most useful. Thanks to Mrs. McSwain for including the full text of these letters, which are the bases of some of the info shown.

The probable family group of Francis Jones/MaryTingnall:

Francis Jones II======MaryTingnall

Nath'l	**Francis III**=**Mary Ridley**	**Matthew III**=**Martha Harwood**	**Britton**
(-c1750)	(c17??-1758)	(c1730 -1756)93 (bef 1708 -)	
		Harwood===Mary Chisman	
		(-9 Feb 1771) | (4 Nov 1730-12 Mar 1781)	

---

[93] Boddie, *Hist* ... VI/93. These dates agree quite well with the Chisman Family Bible (q.v.) which gives the date of b. of Martha's dau Mary as c1730, the year of her (Mary's) m. as 1744, and the d. at age 51 as 1781 [confirming her b. at c1730].

m. 4 Nov | 1744

Ships **Again**   The Exec. Journal *(v. III, 1705-1721, pp 94-5)* also shows for 1706 that **Francis** was one of the masters of merchant ships in the James River. No doubt both he and his father were wealthy merchants, and we can readily believe that they used a vessel for trade with England and Europe. McSwain adds:

> "There are several references [in *English Duplicates* ...] to a ship owner, **Matthew Jones of London,** England in 1700. ... but **Francis Jones,** most certainly his son, had a merchant ship on the James River. ... Matthew [I] Jones , as a big merchant, had to have some source beside local trade for his very great fortune.'[94] [The reference to London might have to do with the ship's registry or a trade route rather than residence of the ship's master].   [Her footnotes refer to Dorman, *York Co.* ...]

The 13 chen of Francis Jones [III] & Mary Ridley: (Francis [III], cousin of Ridley – McSwain /241) and wife Mary Ridley *(from the 1750 w. of FJ)*: , prob not in birth order, were:

1. **Nathaniel** (c1730.-1810) m. c1757 in Johnston Co., NC [*IGI*] **Ann Snickers** (c1737, NC -) of Snicker's Ferry, VA; [Anon]. { *'Anon' = pages in the Genealogy Vertical File at NC State Library by, partly, anonymous writers.*}
2. **Jones:Tignal** (c1735-May 1807) m. c1756 **Penelope Cain** (d. 1826)
3. **Francis** (c1733 to 1750; 1750:<18 yrs). m. **Frances Yancy**
4. **Albridgeton**[50] (d. 1788 {Anon}) m. **Mary Hardy**; chen: **Wm.** (w. 1793), **Jemimah, Penny Hardy, Willis** [*Wake crt recs* (see Appendix I)]
5. **John**[50] m. **Mary Cain,** sister of Penelope (AAW: They had **Willis,** . .. **Jas.. Wm**)
6. **Mary** m. **(Col.) John McCullers.** A dau m. **George Stuart** and had
.. **TJ & George McCullers** bef. 19 Jan 1750 (w. of FJ III)
7. **Judith** m. **(Capt.) Wilson** bef. 19 Jan 1750 (date of w. **of FJ III)**
8. **Ridley** (lived in Halifax Co., NC)
9. **Lucy.** m. **Cpt. Brown**
10. **Bette Day**
11. **Lydia.** M. **Drury Mims**
12. **Jemima**
13. **Matthew** (lived in Halifax Co., NC)

Notes   This Tignal [Sr.] & Penny were parents of **Redding** who m. the widow **Grant (Martha Bustian). Redding & Martha** had **John R. Jones,**

---

[94] Quoting from Mc Swain p. 174, citing the quitrent rolls

grfa of **Susie Gentry** to whom AAW's letters were addressed, and dau **Sarah Redding Jones**.[95] **Martha** had had 1 son, fa of **Judge Grant**. -AAW

This list of the names of the chen in this family corresponds well to their heredity: **Mary** and **Francis** (the names of mother and father), **Albridgeton** and **Tingnall** (the two grandmothers' surnames), **Ridley** (the maternal grandfather's surname), **Nathaniel** and **Matthew** (the two grandfathers' given names), **Lydia** (the mother's eldest sister), and **John** (the father's brother and, interestingly, the name '**Bette Day**' is an almost exact copy of the name of grandmother **Elizabeth Day**. **Jemima** is the name of an aunt. I cannot show any ancestral significance for the remaining names, **Lucy** and **Judith** (unless 'Judith' refers back to the wife of **John Tingnall**).

AAW: A bro of **Ann Snickers** had 1 son (only) who m. **Miss Washington**. Senator **Jas K. Jones** of AR is the son of **NJ** and grson of **MJ**.

The Will of FJ III[96]   At this point we insert in abstract the will of this Francis written in 1750 and pr. 1755, Note that the order of chen named towards the end appears to be the birth order but doesn't include the daus Mary, **Lucy**, and **Judith**.

> To my two sons **Nathaniel** [b. c 1729?] & **Tingnall** my upper track of land on Crabtree Creek in Johnston County, Nathaniel to have the first choice. My son-in-law **John Cullers** shuld run a dividing line in the loer track of my land on Crabtree Creek...for my wife **Mary Jones** [and] my son Nathaniel to chuz one part for my son John Jones. ... and the other part I give to my son-in-law John Cullers.   To my son **Matthew Jones** my land and plantation on Swift Creek in Johnston Co. and five pounds of VA money.   To my son **Francis Jones** my land on Jackit Swamp in Edgecombe Co. at the adge of eighteen years.   I give the plantation whereon I now live and the use of my copper still to my beloved wife **Mary Jones** during her natural life or widowhood and at her deth or ... idy to my son Francis Jones..   To my son **Albridgton** twenty five pounds of VA money for to be raisd out of my personal estate.   To my dau **Judith Wilson** one negro girl.   To my dau **Mary Cullers** one negro boy.   To my dau **Lucy Jones** one negro girl.   To my wife two negro women and blue side saddle   And all the remainder part of my estate both royal and personal here and elsewhere I lev to be equally divided between my beloved wife and my chen as followeth **Nathaniel Jones   Tingnall Jones   Matthew Jones, Albridgton Jones, Lydia Jones   Ridley Jones**[97] **Jemima Jones**

---

[95] *IGI Index*
[96] Edgecombe Co., NC [Grimes, *Abstracts of NC Wills,*] p. 191
[97] This Ridley might be the one whose w. of 1824 is in Halifax Co.

and **Susie**. Appt wife **Mary Jones** and son Nathaniel to be my exors...
19 Jan 1750. Francis Jones [seal]

Info of Dr. Barry Hayes (abstracted): **Francis Jones** may have been the son of the **Nath'l Jones**, surveyor of the highway between Deep Creek and Waters Creek ... at the location of some property that a **Samuel Browne**, quite possibly the **Dr. Samuel Browne** of this [Hayes'] article, patented in 1733. Nath'l Jones followed **Matthew Jones** to the Nottoway Basin where he appears for the 1st time on 3 Feb 1723 as a witness to a deed. Nath'l Jones purchased 200 acres on 24 Mar 1725 (Nugent III 308) at Cypress Swamp, but deeded it to Francis Jones. McSwain (her p.192) discovered this conveyance in a document of 4 Nov 1741, when Francis & wife **Mary Jones** deeded the land before departing for NC; a wit. was Nath'l Jones; this was the one who witnessed a deed in Edgecombe Co.,

Part 3 of Dr. Hayes' article in **JHA News**[98] focuses on the Browne-Jones-Day-Ridley relationships and includes the relationship of Dr. Jesse Browne (w. of 29 Nov 1770 [*S'hampton WB 2 /357*] to **Albridgton Jones**. The latter witnessed the w. of Dr. Browne and was named in the Browne descendancy.

A son of **Francis II, Francis III**, was named a trustee and guardian in an action of 1758 (/461). White, ... /1871 adds about another **Francis** that his w., dated 8 Feb 1841, is on file at Hillsborough in Orange Co, NC, and names son-in-law **Dr. James S. Smith**, husband of his only child, **Delia**, and grdau **Mary R. Smith**. **Delia Smith** made affidavit in Orange Co. (n.d.) aged 64.

Related or Unrelated:

Misc. A Francis Jones appears 9 Dec 1696 in NC's Palatine Court Vol. 01 /472 with the mention: 'At a Palatines Court holden at the House of Frances Jones, Esq ...' No evidence exists to show any relationship.

A Francis Jones (1750 NC-GA) went to GA c1764 with his wife **Elizabeth Huckabee**, 3 chen, and 6 slaves to petition for a grant of land. He had migrated from Isle of Wight Co., VA with his 1st wife, **Mary Robbins**, who had d. He then moved from Cumberland Co., NC. He received 500 acres in GA, and later bought the mill of neighbor **John Lott** [*The Colonial Records of the State of GA*, the session of 6 Mar 1764 (vol.9/130). This **Francis Jones** had a son FJ (according to a fam. tree) who m. **Polly Lanier** (b. 1752); in another tree he is described as 'Sr.', b. c1714, and the son of **Henry**.

---

[98] *6 JHA4*(Fall 2000) /3

The w. of an FJ dated Mar 1774 in GA *(GA Secy of State)* lists 3 sons, **James** who m. **Eliz Mills, FJ, & Phillip**, a grdau **Lavinia**, and exs **JJ** et al.

Another man of this name was b. 6 Aug 1710 and d. either 9 Apr 1785 or 23 Mar 1801 [various family trees]

A Francis Jones is mentioned in the *Ordinances of Convention*, 1776 of the Provincial Congress 22 Nov-23 Dec 1776 [*Colonial and State Records of NC, v. 23/993*] and other related Joneses are appt'd Justices.

A FJ was a CSA private in Com. I, 22nd Reg., VA Infantry. Another was in Com. B, 56th Reg, VA Inf. Another was sergeant in Com. E, 29th Reg., VA Inf. [*Nat'l Park Service*].

In 1799 in Newbern District a petition was entered by the chen of Francis Jones (-1797), namely **Jonias, David, Nancy, Chloe, Amelia Hardy, Nancy, Sally & Leonora**, saying that their fa d. intestate in Apr 1797 possessed of lands in the counties Beaufort, Craven and Casterick [sp?]—*(NC Digital Collections*, State Library of NC). [apparently unrelated-RD]

FJ (1765-) m. **Agnes Thompson** (1767-) in 1789.   *Yates Publishing, U.S. and International M. Recs.1560-1900.*

A FJ (1750 – 1797) m. **Frances Yancy** (1750-1799); [a family tree]

(17 Jan 1750 IoW-18 Sep 1794 Wake), fa FJ (1692-1755), mother **Mary Eliz Ridley** (1706-1784), m. **Susanna Smith** (b. 1727); [fam. tree].

Brunswick Co., VA   Fothergill, *M Recs of Brunswick Co., VA, 1730-1852*   FJ m. **Lucy Simmons** 11 Jan 1799

Chatham   A Francis Jones is enumerated in the *1790 fedcen* for the Hillside District of Wake Co., NC.   And another in Chatham

Edgecombe W. pr. 1755

IoW the settlement of Matthew Jones' est. is mentioned '… **Mr, Portlock,** Francis Jones wives' shares, etc. [Chapman, B. A., *Ws & Admins of I of W Co....1647-1800*, II/151, for 7 Mar 1750.'

Boddie, *17/179*   MJ wi **Nath'l Ridley** vestrymen, St Lukes. Mentions Assembly Order of 1623, 4 locations ex James town. A Francis Jones is mentioned in the *Ordinances of Convention*, 1776 of the Provincial Congress 22 Nov-23 Dec 1776 [*Colonial and State Records of NC, v. 23/993*] and other related Joneses are appt'd Justices.

A FJ was a CSA private in Com. I, 22nd Reg., VA Infantry. Another was in Com. B , 56th Reg, VA Inf. Another was sergeant in Com. E, 29th Reg.,VA Inf. [*Nat'l Park Service*].

In 1799 in Newbern District a petition was entered by the chen of Francis Jones (-1797), namely **Jonias, David, Nancy, Chloe, Amelia Hardy, Nancy, Sally & Leonora**, saying that their fa d. intestate in Apr 1797 possessed of lands in the counties Beaufort, Craven and Casterick [sp?]—(*NC Digital Collections*, State Library of NC). [apparently unrelated-RD]

FJ (1765-) m. **Agnes Thompson** (1767-) in 1789.   *Yates Publishing, U.S. and International M . Recs.1560-1900.*

A FJ (1750 – 1797) m. **Frances Yancy** (1750-1799);   [a family tree]

(17 Jan 1750 IoW-18 Sep 1794 Wake), fa FJ (1692-1755), mother **Mary Eliz Ridley** (1706-1784), m. **Susanna Smith** (b. 1727);   [fam. tree].

Meck.   FJ m. __ **Booth** in Meckl Co. in 1799.   [*VA Co. M. Recs*]

Nansemond Co., VA   *The Vestry Book of the Upper Parish Nansemond Co., VA 1743-1793*

No'ton Co., NC FJ w. 18 Sep 1783 rec Dec 1784

Northumberland, VA   A FJ b. 1750 Northumberland, VA & d. there, m. 8 Dec 1770 in Lancaster, VA^{99} m. Jane Armistead (b. 1750) [*VA, Select Ms., 1785-1940,* /39]

Ratcliff, …   1787 tax Perquimans Co., NC

Nott   In *Nottoway Co. Deed Book II/525* for 1 Oct 1802   FJ is grantee.

Wake   A Francis Jones is enumerated in the *1790 fedcen* for the Hillside District of Wake Co., NC.   And another in Chatham

A **Francis Nathaniel Jones** (13 Jan 1749, NC-8 Feb 1815, White Plains Cemetery, Cary, Wake Co., , NC-1847) [dau of **Burwell Perry and Elizabeth Massey**], and naming the chen **Alfred** (1789-1865) and ***Wesley*** (1794-1865). [In a fam.tree (prob partly copied from Find A Grave)] he was the son of **Evan Jones** and **Eliz. Wells** (b. 1725). This is a suspicious, confusing source; it has as basis an engraved tombstone, which is usually a reliable source of info

---

[99] *VA Ms.*

(although here we don't know if the inscription is readable or has been read correctly), but the accompanying commentary is clearly faulty in mentioning only 2 chen of **Francis Albridgton Jones**, whose w. exists, and citing other info clearly pertinent only to FAJ. Some sources show a Francis m. to Rachel. There is ample confusion about these men & sources.

1790 fedcen FJ in Hillside section

Warwick Another **FJ** was appt'd surveyor in Warwick Co. in 1760 (494).

York In the Hustings Court of York Co., VA, for 26 Nov 1787 Francis Jones is mentioned as making oath in the probate of **Allen Jones'** will.

York #3 Jdmts & Ords 1759-1763 suit 16 Jul 1759 FJ to pay HL for travel.

Another **Jane Armistead** lived in York Co., m. **Edward Armistead**, had ch. **Moss Armistead** [Kinard, June, *York Co., Charles Parish Records, 1648-1789*]. This Jane Armistead m. 8 Dec 1770 in Lancaster Co, VA [*VA, Select Ms. 1785-1940*]}, and resided in Charles Parish [*York Co., VA, Charles Parish Recs, 1648-1789*]

NC Pension Records, a book without author's name, under call letters 975.6 M29n in the Family History Library at Salt Lake City, includes /58 ' Francis Jones, pvt Wake Co., age 79' [dated 1819, thus b. c1740].

In *Abstract of NC Wills, 1690-1760* is the 10 June 1750 w. of **Evan Jones** in Craven Co. The pr. date is shown as Nov 1751. It names sons **Evan, Jas, Roger**, and **Charles**, wife **Ann**. Wits: **Catherine Jones, Wm Flood**, et al. In the same source for 23 Dec 1752, also Craven Co., is another Evan Jones' w., pr. 19 Mar 1753. This Evan is the son, Evan, named in the w. just above (judging from the allusion in both ws. to the plantations). This w. names his son, **Lovick**, dau **Sarah**, wife **Ann**, exs **Thos. Lovick & Roger Jones**. Wits: **Jas. Jones, George Jones, John Taneyhill**. Clerk General Court, Jno. Snead

Francis Albridgton Jones

This name has been the source of much confusion. Often ' Francis A. Jones' is seen, and sometimes simply ' Francis Jones.' As a result, this man can be mistaken easily for his uncle **Francis Jones [II]**. McSwain postulates (her p. 240) that F.A.J. was the son of **John [II]**. She further says that the first son of F.A.J. was **John Jones**. She shows (pps. 241 & ff) several deeds and the 1781 will of F.A.J. (pr.1788) showing without any doubt the existence of the man and citing various sources including *IoW DBk 5*, pps 52 & 154; *DB6, p.232; DB7, pps.256-8; Southampton DB2, p.60; records of*

Nash and Edgecombe Counties, NC, etc. This information ranges from a calculated b. year of 1718-1720 in Warwick County, a m. year of c1740 to **Julian Newsom**, a death date (year of pr.) of 1788, and the names of the chen, **James Alfred, Wesley,** This man might have been the ' Francis A. Jones' listed in Company I, 3rd Reg., VA Cavalry in the Civil War.[102]

The very extensive and informative investigation by **Terri Russ**, RPA, for Preservation North Carolina, Jan 2014, is somewhat flawed by this confusion of names – namely in mistaking **Francis Albridgton Jones** for his uncle. In section 3.3 of the report the name Francis Albridgton Jones is given instead of Francis Jones, and the dates of the lifespan for Francis Albridgton Jones are given incorrectly as c1675-1755. Then we read that he m. **Mary Ridley**, but the wife of Francis Albridgton Jones was **Julian Newsom**. Mary Ridley was the wife of Francis Jones the uncle. This confusion of names casts doubt on the subsequent information in the article about Francis Jones and descendants, and so other sources must be consulted.

F.A. Jones, Related or Unrelated

Rev. **Francis Albritton Jones** (1780 Halifax Co., NC, - Jul 1845, Halifax Co., NC). [U.S. Find a Grave Index1600s-Current]

d. 1788 Nash, NC   Wife **Scion Bass** (1760-1793) or **Julian** __ [family trees]

b. 1692 Island, Accomack, VA, d.1755 Edgecombe, NC. M.1743, Nash,NC. Fa **Matthew Francis Jones,** mother **Mary Elizabeth "Betsy" Ridley Jones** (1706-84) [fam. Tree]

Albridgton, the second son

According to the naming pattern, the 2nd son would be named after the maternal grandfather. That would make Albridgton Jones the 2nd son. Albridgton's will[107] was made 10 Feb 1717, when he was 'Sick and weak' and was probated in Warwick County 5 Jun 1718. A record (/552) shows that he was 'Sub: Sheriff' to Francis 12 May 1715, and that he executed a court order on 12 May 1715--a record that stands alone for him in the fragments of court records except that he had been constable in 1712 ['for the lower

---

[102] *Nat'l Park Service*
(footnotes 137 to 106 not in use)
[107] At the Library of Virginia. The will was returned to Virginia in 2012. No doubt it is one of the items taken out of the County Clerk's office during the Civil War.

pcints'] (209)[108] and then became sub-sheriff under Francis Jones in 1715 (prob with the influence of Francis). The 1712 entry suggests b. c1690 or bef.

He is not listed in ensuing surviving court records of Warwick County as having served in any other office, or on any jury. His name appears in two other items: one in which he is an assignee (/228) and one tentative (not executed) case in which Francis is assignee for him (/255). The paucity of involvement – even as seen in fragmentary court records—lets us believe that **Albridgton** had little interest in governmental matters or possibly that he had some physical or mental deficiency.

His will is interesting first of all in that it was probated in Warwick County. Unlike the men disfavored by primogeniture and had moved away, Albridgton was one of those who remained in Warwick County. His three daus, **Agatha, Martha, & Elizabeth**, were underage in 1717, and since we had estimated his birth year of at c1690 we could guess his age at death at c27. His daus Martha and Agatha might have the names of their aunts—especially Agatha, which is also the name of a dau of **Matthew II**. His (AJ's) wife is **Elizabeth**, but unfortunately her maiden name was not shown in the w. We do not know whether the naming pattern was used here, as both the child's mother and maternal grandmother were Elizabeths. Since no real estate was mentioned in the will, it is perhaps likely that he had none.

The 1717 Will of Albridgeton Jones

In the name of God amen I Albridgton Jones of Warwick County being Sick and weak in body but in perfect sense and memory thanks be to God for it – constitute and appoint this my last will and testament in manner and form following -- Item I give and bequeath my soul unto the hands of Almighty God my body to the Earth to have Christian buriall in sure and sertain hope of [joy]full resurection at the last day Item my [will and] disire is that all my ... debts ... be first payd. Item My will and disire is that ... divided between my loving wife Elizabeth Jones and my three daughters Elizabeth Jones, Martha Jones Agatha[109] Jones and in case that either of my three daughters should die in there minority or without heirs lawfully begotten that th[eir] part to goe to the survivors ... Item My will and desire is that my loving wife have the use of my whole estate both real and personall during her widowhood and that the Estate be not inventoryed till her marage or death and my will and desire is that **Mr. John Wills** and my loving wife

---

[108] Since the item refers to him as a *past* constable, the previous year is more likely to be correct than the year given in the record entry.

[109] Agatha m. **Thomas Harvey** 25 May 1773 [*Ray, Index...*/79]

Elizabeth Jones be my whole and Sole ... and Execut[ors of] this my last will and testament   Witnesseth my hand this 10th february ... [1717]   Alb: Jones sealed

Signed and sealed ...   In the presence of us Cuthbert Hubbard [and] **Michael Cox**   At a court held for Warwick County on Thursday the fifth of June 1718 This will was presented in court by Elizabeth Jones one of the Executors who made oath ... and being provd by the oaths of Cuthbert Hubbard and Michael Cox the witnesses thereto is admitted to record.

Albridgton's death at a young age is again suggestive that he may have had some sort of physical issue.

***

Albridgtons, related or unrelated

Misc.   A family tree gives the b. as 1776 Peru, and the fa's (also Albridgton)

An Albridgton Jones, son of Francis   Jones and Mary Ridley d. c1789—the year his estate records were entered.[110] *[+NC Estate Files]*

Wilson:1953   AJ, Lt. granted 2666 2/3 a. 3 yrs continental line

Accomack   An Albridgton Jones was b. 1692 at Island, Accomack, Va; *[State Records of NC]*:   AJ mentioned [as rep?] 'for Wake' between 1715 and 1776; ditto 1715 and 1791.

Edgecombe   AJ (Edgecombe Co., - May 1788). Son of **John Francis Jones** and Mary Cain. *[My Heritage]*.

Halifax   AJ dec'd,   NJ Jr ex., bef.11 Oct 1792,

An Albritton was enumerated in *1840 in Halifax, NC [fedcen]*,

In the *NC Palatines Court Minutes of 28 Nov 1776*, 'Albritton Jones of Halifax Co. was appt'd First Lt. in **Capt. Gresham Coffield**'s Company in the first Battalion of Volunteers ...'

NSDAR, *Roster...*/393, 394   AJ (Brittain) in Continental Line (Rev. War)

---

[110] *NC, Will and Probate Records, 1665-1998.* .

IoW AJ's w. 1787 Isle of Wight Co., VA [**Allen Jones**?] Fa: Francis (w. 1750); uncle: **Matthew II**; grfa: **Matthew [I]**; wife: **Mary**

AJ pr. in Isle of Wight 3 Jun 1756 [*VA Land, M., and Pr. Records, 1639-1850*].

A Britton Jones d. c1770 in Isle of Wight Co. (pr. 3 Jan 1771) [*VA Land, M., and Pr. Records, 1639-1850*]. S.a. *Great Book of IoW Co., trns.* /224 [orig /45]. The same source gives **Albridgton** d. 28 Jan. S.a. Brittain in IoW 1759 [LVA: Wills #46]. A 'Britain' is listed as a son in the w. of **Samuel Jones** [*VA, Land M., and Probate Recs, 1639-1850*, and *Great Book trns.*/225 {orig. 74}].

Boddie *17/284* shows the d. as 26 Nov 1787 at Wake, and the wife as **Mary Hardy**. [Anon says he d. in 1788]. The fa: **Francis** (w. 1750), an uncle **MJ II**, gr'fa: **Matt I**.

AJ's chen: Wm, **Willis, Jemima, Penny Hardy**.

AJ Apr 1773 *[Fee Bk ,V. 1, image 21, IoW Co.]*

An Albridgton Jones is called 'Britton' in the w. of his fa., Matthew II (see); he made his w. on 22 Sep 1784 in Southampton Co., VA with a codicil of 12 Dec 1785. An AJ, maybe the same man, d. in Wake c1789 [*NC Wills and Probate recs 1665-1998*]. He was b. in Isle of Wight Co. c1718, m. (1) **Elizabeth Simmons**, (2) **Mrs. Mary Wilson**, widow, bef 1750, and (3) Mrs. Mary Simmons **on 19 Feb 1770**.[111] McSwain cites a passage in the Southampton Co. *Minute Bk 1749-1754 /6* which grants Albridgton letters of adm. on the estate of his fa; this indicates that his mother, Elizabeth had d. (bef 1749). This man's will names sons **William, Matthew and Albridgton**. McSwain also provides the names of the daus **Mary (m. Benjamin Jarrell), Agatha (m. Thomas Harvey),**[112] **Ann (m. Gen. Lawrence Baker), and Elizabeth** (m. [1] **Miles Harvey** and [2] **Benjamin Baker**. McSwain cites Chapman & Knorr), Ms. of Southampton ... pp 28, 29, & 32. It is interesting that the name Agatha is given to one of his chen because both a sister and an aunt were Agathas. It is also interesting that he makes a bequest to Ann Simmons, probably a relative of one of his wives, and that among his sons are yet another Albridgton and another Matthew.

---

[111] See article by Dr. Hayes in [JHA2/3], Chapman's *Wills;*, & Knorr, *M. Bonds* /63].

[112] S.a. Hathaway,...*III/386* Agatha m. 25 May 1773 Thos. Harvey

A tree has the b. as 13 Jul 1792, the m. as 28 Jan 1813 in Isle of Wight Co., VA; the residence as 1830 Montgomery, TN, the d. as 25 Oct 1833 in TN, the prnts as **Albridgton Jones** (1749-1809) & **Mary Simmons**. (1752-1794), and the spouse as **Sarah Ann Applewhite** (1796-1884).

(**AJ** cont'd)   bonds: IoW 1 Jan 1755, 3 Jun 1756 [*All Court, Land, Wills and Financial ...(VA)]*.

AJ ex. for **George Portlock**, mention 3 Jun 1756 [*All Court, Land, Wills and Financial ...(VA)]*.

Nansemond Co., VA *The Vestry Bk of the Upper Parish* 15 Nov 1762 'for keeping the ferry over Notaway'

Clerks' Fee Books   (Gen. Soc. Hampton)   4 May 1774 fee action

Clerks' Fee Books microfilm p. 378   AJ ex of **MJ** suit 1795

Clerks' Fee Books microfilm pp. 54, 189, 610, 667, 725   records 1791-1800

So'ton   AJ to **George Briggs** of Sussex Co. Deed of 100 a. adj Nottoway Swamp. So'ton Co. 10 Feb 1768, [*So'ton Co. DB 3 pp 19-21*], US GEN Web

AJ et al 240 a. 19 Feb 1755 [*So'ton Co. DB 2 60-61*]

Index of Rev War Pensions in the Nat'l Archives, lists several Joneses with familiar first names who lived long enough to have received a pension or bounty-land warrants: /297 **Albridgton Jones**, VA, in 1807 a resident of Southampton Co., VA; BLWT [bounty land warrant] /359-200.[113]

6T276   Col. Britton Jones mentioned in 1813 wi wife Polly Calvert. Names fa MJ.

AJ, single, age 46, laborer, d. 1823 in Southampton Co. c1823. [*VA Deaths and Burials, 1853-1912*]   An Albritton Jones d. c1802

AJ will So'ton 1786 [LVA: Wills]

AJ in *1820 FEDCEN* for Southampton, VA: 2 males under 10, 1 26-44, 1 45 or over; 4 females under 10, 1 10-15, 2 16-25.c

Southampton Co. *[LVA, Land Office Patents #38]*

A tree gives his d. as 19 Jul 1786 at Southampton, VA.

AJ from **Richd Williams** 200 a. S side of Blackwater Swamp *[So'ton Co. DB 2 pp 63-4]*

AJ (Nottoway Parish) (from **J. Wright**) 170 + 17 a. 11 Jan 1791 *[So'ton Co. DB 7 pp 455-57]*

AJ   1780 w.

Col. AJ m. to **Polly Calvert** in 1813 [6T276]

VA Genealogist XXV/2   AJ sec 13 Oct 1796

Wake   On 2 Mar (May?) 1785   AJ m. *[Wake Co. M Bonds /261]* **Cada Barts**

AJ in Hillsboro Dist., in the *1790 fedcen* (and see other fedcens).

AJ is in the 1790 fedcen for Wake, NC and 1820 for Southampton, VA.

An Albritton was enumerated in 1880 in Wake Forest, NC [fedcen].

On 1 Apr 1780 he was in Wake *[NC Land Grant Files, 1693-1960]*.

Brittain Jones, Pvt .... Wake Co., age 79 [in 1819, thus b. c1746 *[NC Pension Records /58 –]*

AJ, Esq apptd justice 'for Wake' *[NC Provincial Congress 23 Dec 1776, v. 23, pp 985-1000]*

AJ d. bef 1789; orphs were **Willis** (d. bef 1792), **Penny H.** (c1787-post 1799), **William,**   **& Jemima**. Gdn was NJ Sr. Wake.   NJ, Jr. bound also.

AJ's orphs incl **William & Jeremiah** [*Wake court minutes Bk 2 /37*]

AJ ordered to jury duty c1795 [*Wake court minutes Bk 3 /89*]

AJ vs **James Jones,** Feb 1802 [*Wake court minutes Bk5 /76*]

The *NC, Land Grant Files, 1693-1960* shows 1 Apr 1780 for Wake, NC, for **Albridgton Jones**

Military   An Albrighton Jones is shown as adjutant in the U.S. Revolutionary War Rolls, 1775-1783 /136 [*National Archives and Records Administration* microfilm M246].   And   List *of Rev Soldiers of VA, Dept. of Archives and History,* 1911: AJ adj. 4 mentions for AJ.   And *US Rosters of Rev War Soldiers and Sailors, 1775-1783:* mil. Service 11 Mar 1776; 4th VA, 15th VA, 11th, 2nd Lt., 1st Lt., Adjutant. D. in VA.   And [*Recs of the Rev War, The Military and Financial Correspondence of Distinguished Officers,* prisoners of war, 1858]: mentions also Samuel Jones & AJ Adjutant, between 1775 and 1783. *NC List of Fed Pensions ...Rev War v. 22/71* show a 'Brittain' and a 'Britton' as privates

[*NC Pension Records*], a book without author's name, under call letters 975.6 M29n in the Family History Library at Salt Lake City, includes /58 'Brittain Jones by calculation]. [*LVA Archives, Land Grants*], lists Albridgton Jones as grantee 25 May 1734.   McSwain, citing Heitman, *Historical Register* ..., describes his military service more fully (her /236). Other men named Albridgton (or variants) in the 18th century will be apparent from other military records, many of which defy identification as to specific persons: In the *NC Palatines Court Minutes of 28 Nov 1776,* 'Albritton Jones of Halifax Co. was appt'd First Lt. in **Capt. Gresham Coffield's** Company in the first Battalion of Volunteers ...'

'Brittain Jones, Pvt .... Wake Co., age 79 [in 1819, thus b. c1746 [*NC Pension Records /58*]. *US Rev War Rolls, 1775-1783:* '**Britn Jones**' 1778. *FHL Collections,* VA Hist. Soc., Richmond. AJ mentioned 'in southern army'.   *Index of Rev War Pensions* in the Nat'l Archives, lists several Joneses with familiar first names who lived long enough to have received a pension or bounty-land warrants: Albridgton Jones., VA, in 1807 a resident of Southampton Co., VA; BLWT [bounty land warrant] /359-200.[114]
      /298 Britain/ Britton Jones, enl[isted] in Pitt Co., NC; d. 17 Apr

---

(footnotes 113-11 not in use)

1847; [he was] 57 in 1818 [thus b. c1761; note date problems--RD]. White, *Genealogical Abstracts of Revolutionary Pensions File* II (F-M)/1867, he assigned his rights to bounty land on 20 Jan 1807 to one Thomas D. Harris in Southampton Co., VA. Saffel .../256 AJ Lt. c1777 wi Cpt John C. Jones, M.D. et al. Continental Army. Half pay & bounty land

***

Nathaniel third son?

This man is probably a son of Matthew I and Elizabeth Albridgton; he is definitely related in some way; he could have been the son of a brother of Matthew I if the naming pattern is thought to apply here. The appearances of this name in the fragmentary Warwick County Court records begins in 1696 (/4) with an order of attachment (to his belongings)[116]; that would give Nathaniel a likely birth year of around the 1670s. He is mentioned as sub-sheriff in 1709 (/12). Additional items from 1698 to 1714 are suits (one involving 3000 lbs. of tobacco!), appraisals, a 'surveyor' of roads (betw Deep & Waters Creeks), & a bond. (They are on pps. 59, 64, 90, 92, 99, 126, 196, 201, 204-5, 207, 210, & 228 of Dunn:2008.). There are no entries after Mar 1714 for a Nathaniel Jones in existing Warwick County court records. It is likely that further records will be found in other VA counties or in NC.

Related or Unrelated

Misc. NJ orph of NJ. Acct 1826-38

6T143 NJ d. 3 Jun 1702

Wills, Wake w. of **NJ (CT)**

NJ, Jr. pet 1838. Bk /6 1819 order to div. persal. est. of NJ amongst heirs. [p.16] **Allen** sum'd to testify for NJ, adm 1818 [*Bk A/126* and *NC Est Files.* [p.88] Dower: lands of **William Jones** & **Albridgton Jones** -- where John Jones lived. NJ d. intestate c1816

Hathaway, .../94 NJ m. 31 Dec 1796 **Polly Davis** minister's return

NJ's grchen via **Burwell & Mary Palmer**: [p. 24] **Jacob G. Walker** m. **Louisa E. John A. Pulliam** m. **Amelia** [in TN], **Rachel J.** d. 7 Sep 1821;

---

[116] Nine attachments (to his living estate) occur in these records; nine of them involve debt where Nathaniel is the deft. His reliability about debts looks poor.

Jacob was in Chatham Co., NC; bondsmen on will of Nat incl **Burwell Perry, Kim Jones** & **Seth Jones**

Chowan

NJ d. 1817 intestate (Matilda, widow) Chowan Co. *Bk B /108 & /97 & 77 &/45,132, 122.* re orph of

NJ orph of NJ. Acct 1826-38

NJ, Jr. pet 1838. *Bk /6 1819* order to div. persal. est. of NJ amongst heirs. [p.16] **Allen** sum'd to testify for NJ, adm 1818 [*Bk A/126* and *NC Est Files*].

Johnston A NJ d. testate 20 Dec 1829 (*NC, Estate Files* – 29 pages); wife **Polly**. Chen: **Willis T.** (d. 1852 in MS), **Julia Jones:**, **Elizabeth, Henry** (d. intestate unm. 1858 in Johnston Co.), **Jane, Leroy, Wm**, **John Leach, ex.** [Crt of P & Q S, Nov term 1858]. **Polly** d. in 1858; **Leroy Jones** became ex of NJ.

So'ton Nathaniel A. Jones, d. at age 25 on 19 Jul 1862. B. c1837. Fa NJ, mother **Nancy**. *VA Ds. and Burials, 1853-1912*

Chapman, *So'ton Co. Ws.* NJ justice 8 Jun 1749

Wake Nathaniel Jones (Jr?) (WP) d. 1815 testate [*NC Estate Files*— 164 pages], m. **Rachel.** Chen: **Seth, Joel L[ane?], Burwell, Timothy, Henry** (m. **Nancy**), <u>**Wesley, Amelia, Temperance, Patsy, Sally, Helena**</u>, [underlined were under age], Joseph Alston (m. **Elizabeth**), James Palmer (m. **Patsy** or '**Polly**'). Land purchased of **Tignal Jones**, shff, adj **Henry Jones** & **Redding** & **John C. Jones**. Son (of **Nathaniel Jones, [Jr?]**: **Tim. Watton Jones**. [p.10]: **Alfred** in Fayette Co. TN in 1848, demanding share of est of Rachel, decd. [p.13] 1850 petition by **Elizabeth Alston** to sell land [she was wife of **Joseph A. Alston**] vs John Lane (wife Sally) & **Alfred Jones**

p. 19: **Nathaniel Jones** had 4 sons & 7 daus incl. **Helena Jeffrys**, p.21: **Mary Palmer**, decd [her chen: **Nat J. Palmer, John C., James ..., Laura** m. **Jacob G. Walker**; **Rachel Jones, Helen Jones** were chen of Burwell.

NJ's grchen via Burwell & Mary Palmer: p. 24: **Jacob G. Walker** m. **Louisa E.** , **John A. Pulliam** m. **Amelia** [in TN], **Rachel J.** d. 7 Sep 1821; Jacob was in Chatham Co., NC; bondsmen on will of Nat incl **Burwell, Perry, Kim Jones** & **Seth Jones**. /19 Chen of NJ (WP) heirs to 512 a. and grist mill of Crabtree tract by w. of Rachel.

NJ, Sr. (WP). W. pr. Feb 1810. NJ's wife was **Anna B.** Sons: **Nath'l, m. Annah __, Albridgton, Henry m. Peg Kimbrough;** Daus: **Barbee, Polly Paxton (2nd m);** bro, **Matthew Jones.** grchen: **A. Ben Wooten** .

Wills, Wake   NJ Jr (WP)   W. 7 Sep 1811 chen: **Timothy, Seth, Joel Lane, Burwell Perry, Wesley.** Bros-in-law: **Jeremiah, Burwell Perry**

Wills Wake   NJ Sr. w. 7 Sep 1811? Names **Phillip, Fanning, Ridley, Henry.**   Kim alive.

Wills, Wake   NJ (CT) w. 31 Dec 1828   wife: **Elizabeth**; son: **Kim.**, bro: **Henry**, nc: **Elizabeth Young**, dau of **Hen. Warren?**, fa of NJ **Dan.**

The **NJ**, son of **Kimbrough Jones & Mary P. Hogan**, b. 19 Dec 18??, d. 20 Apr 1860 (*NJ Bible 1758-1915*).

Wm, son of **Kimbrough Jones & Mary P. Hogan**, d. 5 May 1865 (*NJ Bible 1758-1915*).

Wills Wake   **Kim. Jones** w. 11 Mar 1866 wife: **Mary W. __**, sons-in-law: **Thos, Kim Davis;**   sons: **Kim., Wm, Henry;** 2 Daus: **Mittie, Pattie E.** other daus: **Mary Davis, Nipper.**   lists gr'chen

NJ son of NJ b. 27 Oct 1758 at Crabtree Creek, Orange Co. {later Wake Co. (*NJ Bible 1758-1915*).

The NJ who d. 1828, m. 10 May 1821 (3) **Mary W. Warren.** Their chen incl a son **Kim. Jones** (*Crabtree Jones Papers, 1771-1940, from State Archives of NC).*

NC Co. Marriages, 1762-1979   NJ to **Eliz. Powell** 21 Aug 1781, to **Grizeal Kimbrough** 11 May 1782, to **Betsy Utley** 22 Aug 1797

Haun, ...*Lnd Entries* heirs of NJ   Redding, NJ (CT) wits

Chen of NJ (WP) heirs to 512 a. and grist mill of Crabtree tract by w. of Rachel.

John Jones

No recs exist to tell us which John Jones is which, but there is sufficient documentation to be sure of definite connections to this family line.   The first question is whether or not there was a son named John in the family of **Matthew I and Eliz. Albridgton.**

The first appearance of the name in the existing Warwick Co. colonial recs was in 1713 -- which suggests a b. of c1692 or before--a birthyear perhaps more suggestive of a gr'son than a son. But the real birthyear could well be earlier than the calculated one, and the range of birthyears in the family could have been large—especially considering the mostly unknown number of girls and the totally unknown possibility of still-borns. But the most compelling consideration is the abundance of records concerning the presence in county affairs of this JJ and JJ Jr. We believe that the JJ 'of 1713 'was indeed a son of **Matthew I.**

The activities of this JJ in county affairs extend to at least 1762 (the last year in the existing 1748-62 fragment), so his d. was 1762 or later (/614). He apparently had a son, **John Jr.** Jr.'s b. was c1728 or before—again reckoning an age of at least 21 at the time of his first jury service. However, the name ' John Jones Jr.' does not appear in the fragments after 7 Oct 1756 (/436), and we cannot know whether the fa or the son had died, in short whether the entries after 1756 refer to the man previously known as sr. or to the jr. We do not have any records that clarify this matter.

We do find the mention of other JJs including a *son* of Matthew [I] and Eliz. Albridgton (according to McSwain) and purported fa of **Francis Albridgton Jones** (see section on Francis), plus a *gr'son* of that JJ, also called John Jones.

As for the English naming pattern, it is possible that the name John refers back to an IoW brother of his fa.. Boddie, *Seventeenth* ... and especially *9Tyler/283* show many entries for a John Jones, Sr., cooper, in the 17th century in a date range of c1645-1697[117] in IoW Co., and Newman, writing in Tylers, suggests a connection to Matthew I – a distinct possibility. This JJ left his w. in IoW 1697, and had a son **John Jones** (see Hayes' article in *JHA*).[118] He also had a son **Abraham** who had a son **Matthew Jones.** Hayes cites Chapman, *IoW W.s* pp 37, 186, 197, 198]. (S.a. Chapman, *Ms.* /27 for m. to **Mrs. Wollard** [Bk 2/69]). The Matthew he mentions might be named for an uncle--namely Matthew I (again referring to the same naming pattern). But 'John' is a biblical name and also could be simply a traditional English name.

---

[117] The IoW John's w. was 1697 (s.a. *IoW Co. Recs, 1634-1951*, image 60 of 164), dated Jul 1697. Names chen **Abraham, Ann Barnes, gr-son John Barnes. Wife Ann.**
[118] *7JHA* (Winter 2001) /4

But significant for any accuracy in a genealogical project are the special problems of *colonial* usage: Sr. and Jr. did not necessarily denote fa-son as in modern usage, but sometimes simply meant 'older-younger'; if Sr. d. then Jr. would then be Sr., ipso facto, and a suffix would cease to exist for that person. In short, a John Jones, Jr. would become simply 'John Jones' upon the d. of Sr.   In one instance (/617 -- 1749) the records show a Jr., *and* a 'younger' as jurors. The names of the jurors in that matter number exactly 12, so it's not likely that there's any error. 'Younger' does not appear again in the fragments. And **John Jones Sr.** and **J^r** were both cited, in different entries, as executors of the same estate -- a seeming impossibility that points to a lack of precision in recording or perhaps an arrangement totally unknown to us.

There are no mentions of a JJ in the existing colonial court records for Warwick County before 1713, but the JJ in the minutes of 1713 (/ 215) shows him as the maker of a security bond with **Francis Jones**—suggesting adulthood and prob a man of some means. He was on the Commission of Peace in 1727 (McElwaine IV/156), JP in 1729 (/136), and Sheriff of Warwick Co. in 1735 (McElwaine IV/349 and Cognets p. 35).

Here we face a 'road bump' in that a John Jones was sworn shff in 1751 with John Jones Jr. appt'd under-shff (/339). These appointments could be the '1713 JJ' and his son, but we cannot be positive; the interval of 16 years in his two positions of sheriff is not comforting. The 1751 situation, however, is the result of a commission by the president of the colony allowing JJ to be shff '*during pleasure,*' so it appears to be a matter of personal choice that the '1713 JJ' and his son *chose* to hold forth in the years 1751-1753 (/624-5), and it may be that JJ saw that as a time to bestow upon his son a position in government. Both men also served together on the bench 3 Jan 1756 (/612).

Another JJ d. in Warwick Co. before 6 Feb 1752 when his wife, **Mary**, became administratrix of his estate; [his estate appraisement was returned to court on 5 Oct 1752 (/363)].   Their chen were **Ann & Frances.** Ann (or Anne) m. **Robert Lucas** and their chen were **Tom** (evidently the eldest), **Sally, Nancy, Robt Gervase,** *John Jones Lucas* (bef 6 Jul 1758-), **Lucy,** and **Elizabeth.**[119] All the chen were underage in 1781. A John Jones, prob the same man, was on the court in 1748 (/289). Several items give us a fair view of this matter:

    1.   [/347   Feb 1752:] On the Motion of **Mary Jones**...Certificate is Granted her for Obtaining letters of Administration on the Estate of

---

[119] The w. of Robt Lucas 20 May 1781, pr. Mar 1782 in Warwick Co. Crt. (copy by Richard Cary). [Found in *York Co. recs* and now at *LVA*. See the full will below].

her dec'd Husband **John Jones** She gave Bond with **Harwood Jones & Servant Jones** her Securities in the Penalty of two Thousand Pounds Sterling ...

[/353   4 Jun 1752:] **Anne Jones & Frances Jones** Orphans of **John Jones** dec'd being admitted chose **Mary Jones** their Guardian, Whereupon she together with **James Goodwin & John Jones jun**ʳ her Securities ... Bond in the Penalty of two Thousand Pounds.

2. *Then note the action of friend, **Robert Lucas**, to expedite the probate process.*

[/370   1 Mar 1753:] On the Motion of **Robert Lucas** It is Ordered ... settle acct ... of **John Jones** ...to allot the Estate of **John Jones** dec'd and return the Division to the next court.

3. *Next the indenture of m. to her dau, **Ann** (or Anne) and the belated dowry award.*

[/373   1 Mar 1753:] An Indenture of Marriage Articles between **Robert Lucas** of the first Part **Mary Jones** Widow, of the second Part and **Anne Jones** an Infant Orphan of **John Jones** dec'd of the third Part was proved by the Oaths **of Servant Jones Harwood Jones** and **John Chisman** three of the Witneses thereto And Ordered to be Recorded

[/465   6 Jul 1758] Mary Jones & Frances, infant, by Harwood Jones vs Robert Lucas & John Lucas, infant....widow's dowry

4. *Then the d. of the widow **Mary** and the action of another friend, **James B. Southall** and his subsequent m. to the other dau, **Frances**.*

[/525   2 Jul 1761   On the Motion of **James Southal** and his making Oath according to Law, Certificate is Granted him for obtaining Letters of Admon on the Estate of **Mary Jones** deceased

Ordered that **James Dowsing, Laurence Haynes William Cary and Higginson Wade** ...do appraise in current Money the Slaves & personal Estate of Mary Jones, dec'd.

5. *Then Anne d.*

[/532   7 Jan 1762:] On the Motion of **Robert Lucas** ... Certificate is Granted him for obtaining Letters of Admon on the Estate of his dec'd Wife **Anne Lucas** Whereupon he together with **Harwood Jones** G^t enter'd into & acknowledged Bond in the Penalty of two thousand Pounds for his due & faithful Admon of the said Estate

Robert Lucas was close to the family of **John Jones** and his wife **Mary** from at least 1752, when her husband John d.; Lucas was an executor for **Scervant Jones** in IoW Co. as late as 1773[120] in which year, on 25 Oct, he was appt'd Sheriff in Warwick Co.[121] His w. names his son **John Jones Lucas**:

> *1781 Will of Robert Lucas:* In the Name of God Amen I Robert Lucas do ...[no words following]   Item I give unto my Son **Tom Lucas** Part of my Tract of Land including the Dwelling House, out Houses orchard _ where I now live bounded by the Bottom between this _ where Burt lived thence from the Head of said Bottom to the large Hiccory [sic] by the Road thence along the said road to the Head of the Simmon tree Bottom thence down said Bottom to the Mill Pond then down the Mill Pond to Mr. Dowsing's line thence along the said Line to Skif's Creek I likewise give him 25 Acres in the Briery Branch joinging [sic] **General Nelson**'s to be laid off by a due North Line I likewise give him Shpney [sp?] & Venus, 10 Head Cattle, 10 Head Sheep 10 Head of Hogs 1 Bed & Furniture & 1 Sgl [?] Folding Table The rest of my Land I desire may be sold for Tobo or what my Executor shall think best and the produce of the said Sale to be equally divided amongst my three Sons or the Survivors of them Vizt & **John Jones Lucas** And I give my Slaves Stock and all my personal Estate to be sold & the Proceeds be equally divided amongst my children **Sally Nancey Robert Gervase Lucy Elizth** and **John** or the Survivors of them for their Support & Maintainance [sic] at the Discression [sic] of Guardians I appoint [my friend] **Doctr Galt** Guardian to my three Boys their to bring them up as He thinks [proper] on their Estates and my Friend **Mr. [?] Trebell** Guardian of my Dau[gh]ters with the like Limitations I constitute & appoint Friend **Col. Edward Harwood** ... **Doctr Galt**[122] my Exor[s] of this my last Will and Testament this 20th Day May 1781 [?] ...   [Lu]cas

Meanwhile **James Barrett Southall** (c1726-bef. 1787)[123] took an interest in this Jones family, married Frances, raised 8 chen, lived in Williamsburg, (druggist in Wmsbg ?), ran Raleigh Tavern for several years, and was bu. at Mulberry Island Church (probably the 'upper church' mentioned in the

---

[120] *Dunn: 2016* /19
[121] *Journals of the Council* ... VI/546
[122] A **James Galt** was a keeper of the insane hosp. to 1800 [*Rockefeller Lib PH0240*].
[123] Wikitree

fragments of Warwick Co. records) in 1787. Frances was bu. there c1780, and their son, **Peyton Randolph Southall**, was bu. there in 1812.[124]

Graphically this was the situation:

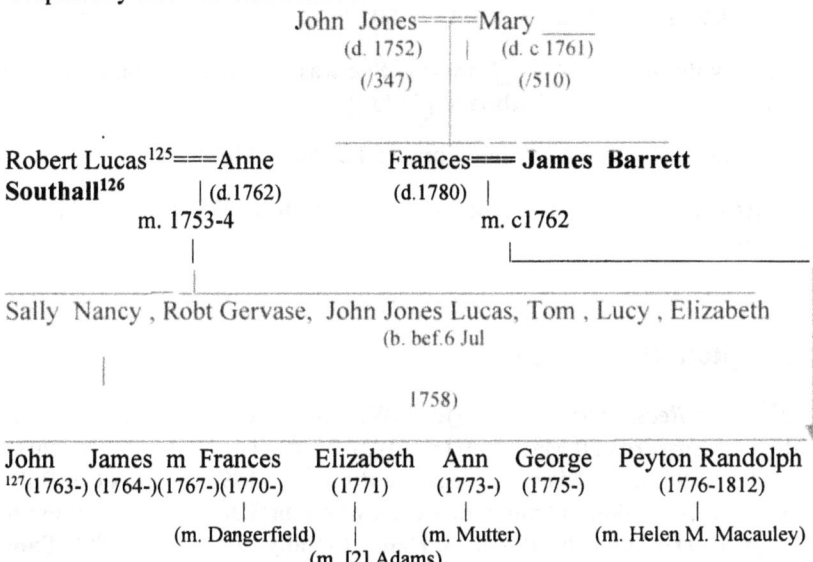

There is at least one other **John Jones** to include in the line from **Matthew I,** and he is the son of **Francis** III (his w. of 1750-1755), the inheritor of land on Crabtree Creek in Wake Co., NC. [See section on FJ]

Several court records from 1756 (pp 416, 422,430-1) identify the wife of one John Jones as Constance. The JJ who d. in 1752 might be 'Senr,' A JJ, magistrate for Warwick Co. on 5 Feb 1756, was domiciled in Hampton (/516), and one (Jr.) a resident of Warwick Co. 5 Aug 1756 (/432), was probably the same person in Warwick Parish in 1754 (/383), but there are no records to connect one to another.

---

[124] *Dunn:2019* pp. 2-3
[125] Will of Robert Lucas of 20 May 1781, pr. Mar 1782 in Warwick County Court; found in York records but now at LVA.
[126] *WikiTree.com,* Richmond Standard, York Chancery 16 Aug 1763 (re estate of Mary). He was under age in 1748, lived in Williamsburg, m. 1761?, d. 1787, bu. at Mulberry Island Church.
[127] The data on the chen is from *45WM29.*

61

Related or Unrelated

Misc   *NC List of Fed Pensions* shows JJ as pvt in Rev War. *Guardian Recs of IoW Co., v. 1 (1766-1782)* show **Mary, John, Wm, Allen, and Frederick** as orphans of JJ Aug 1778-80.

JJ Sr.'s wife **Mary** m. (2) **__Roberts**. She was called **Aunt Pollie Roberts** by **Dr. George Miles Hubbard** [*7T135*]

JJ Sr. uncle of **John A. Jones**   prnts ; **JJ, Mary Hubbard**

Bockstruck   JJ militia 13Jul 1756 age 31 (b. c1725; enl Nov 1755 at Richmond

EEC JJ 1756

Hampton   JJ 5 Feb 1756

IoW *Tax Recs, Marriages, etc* (for IoW) show several Jones ms.: **Betsy** m. **Michael Edwards** 20 May 1789 (p. 33), p. 36 **Lydia** to **Solomon Newman** 25 May 1795, p. 38 **Mary to Benj. Banks** Jul 13 1795, p. 39 **NJ to Polly Davis** 31 Dec 1796, **Thomas to Eliz. Chapman** 5 Jan 1797, **Thomas to Peggy Morrison** 6 Feb 1795, p. 40 **Henry to Sally Lewis** 7 Apr 1800, **Sam. to Eliz. Jordan** 30 Apr 1800, p. 42 **Joseph to Eliz. Mallicote** 21 Mar 1808, **Thomas to Sarah Davidson** 8 Aug 1807, **John to Anne Stringfield** 31 Aug1807, p. 44 **Eliz. to Sampson Banks** 4 Oct 1814, and **John R. to Margaret Harrison** 21 Mar 1813. [Note the error of 3 Thomases.]

JCC   *fleet Ser 1/IV 36-7*   JJ land; Milford 30 Jan 1867, 'Lowfield' in ECC. He res at Milford bef war. Deed 24 Dec 1866; son: **Pembroke.** One of the lands 'belonged to his (JJ:s) fa. S.a. *WB I/16*

Nansemond Co., VA   *The Vestry Book of the Upper Parish Nansemond Co., VA 1743-1793* JJ ex for **NJ**   w. 1800

Nash   A JJ d. 1793 in Nash Co., NC leaving sons **Bretain & Lazarus** [*NC Est Files*]

A JJ who d. 1794 had 2 sons, **John & Willie** Ex. was **Judith Jones** [*NC Estate Files – Nash Co.*]

Sussex   *SuxCH M. Index #7*   JJ m. **Eliz Binns** 1758

Sux CH M. Index #9   Binns Jones m. 1781 Eliz. Cargill

Wake   Dr. John Ridley Jones is listed in the *Pedigree Resource File* as the son of **Redding and Martha Bustian;** wife **Martha Lane**; chen **Martha Anne, Mary Louise, Catherine Ella**; b. c1810.

JJ esq apptd Lt Col of Wake Co. militia 25 Apr 1778 [*v. 12/600*]

A JJ was shff in 1753 (/370)

A JJ d. bef 2 Mar 1761 (/519)

A JJ d. bef 1 Mar 1753 Robt Lucas moved to settle est of JJ

Wills Wake   J. C. J. w. 11 Sep 1808, pr May 1810. Mother: **Penny**, others: **John J. Briggs, Fanning Jones, Absalom Alston.** "**Penny** was dau of **Westwood**"

Warwick   A John Jones   apprs. d. bef. 5 Mar 1761 (519) in Warwick; **Mary,** wife of JJ on his d.   J & HJ secs. (347) 6 Feb 1752.

Prob Warwick: "**Martha Jones Ironmonger** late wife of JJ…(sonJohn Jones Jr]" – 1722 [in *VA Gleanings in England* in *11V75 (Jul 1903)].* Same source p 76: **Eliz.,** sister of **Robert Jones** [1681?]

1810 fedcen for War. Co.   **John Jones Jr**   2 fem. 26-45, one under 10; 3 males under 10, one 26-45 , no slaves

1810 fedcen for War. Co.   JJ 1 male 45 up; 1 fem under 10, two 26-45

VA Colonial Soldiers 4 Sept 1755 :   **John Jones Jr, Cpt of the lower foot.**

6T48   JJ age 61 d. 20 Jun 1824 [b. c1763], justice of Warwick, served in Rev. [b. c1763]. Left widow, son.

JJ of War. Co. (441) 1757

Cpt of Lower Foot 1755

Settlemnt of est of **John [Jones] Lucas** not returnd 3 Apr 1729 (132-3)

A JJ was shff in 1753 (/370)

A JJ d. bef 2 Mar 1761 (/519)

A JJ d. bef 1 Mar 1753 **Robt Lucas** moved to settle est of JJ
McGhan & Bentley   JJ d. 7 Feb 1824

York   *York Deeds, etc. 1672-76/541*   JJ apptd poa 24 Apr 1673

Order Bk4 (1774-84) /380   JJ gdn of **John Wills** l6 Sep 1783

York Lnd Causes 1746-1769/214   JJ late of York, ref to Warwick   d. intestate 1766

*York Ws 23/*679   JJ dec'd   inv 1803

York Orders   JJ from War,   wit.19 Mar 1820

York Orders 1820-1825   JJ late shff of War. Suit 19 Mar 1823. Jury incl **William Jones**

S[c]ervantJones[128]

This name enters the Jones genealogy when Matthew II m. **Frances Servant** abt 1712.[129] She was the dau of French Hugenot **Bertrand Servant** who was naturalized in 1698, lived 38 years in ECC, was JP and d. there in 1707 at age 66.[131] This dau m. 1) **John George**[132] (b. c1672-1736, d. intestate bef. mid-1711) and 2) Matthew II. bef. 8 Feb 1712. [Chapman, *Eliz Co. Ws*.] The Servant name (sometimes spelled 'Servent') continues through many generations in the **Matthew Jones** families to at least 1854, when **Rev. Scervant Jones** (3 Apr 1785-3 Apr 1854) was bu. at Bruton Parish Church Cemetery in Williamsburg, VA.[133] [**'Hellcat Billy'** was his nephew.] Rev. SJ's wife was **Ann Timson** [Buckner?] of York Co.

---

[128] The "c" was inserted into the Servant name when it was a *first* name but not when it was a middle name, apparently. to preclude any confusion with the common noun.

[129] *Chapman, Wills ... of ECC* /16. **Frances George** was also named by her sister in Rebecca's will of 1697. [Fn 130 not in use]

[131] From Elizabeth *City County ('ECC') Wills and Administrations, 1689-1800* pp. 82-83. Will pr. 18 Nov 1707 & 19 Feb 1707. *Deeds, Wills & Orders, 1704-1730*, Pt. 2 (Reel 5). S.a. *27W2/136* and *9W/123-4*.

[132] **John George** was ex. of estate of Bertrand. John's cousin was **John Brantley**. The m. license of John and Frances was issued 16 Jun 1696 [*Chapman, op.cit./161*. The Georges apparently had a dau, Frances, bef Bertrand d. in 1707 [*Wills & Admins of ECC,1688-1800*].

[133] *'Find a Grave'* index. He m. **Ann Timson** c1805 [*Ancestry.com*]. York Co. recs show an 1817 deed by SJ & Nancy Timson (*bk. 8 /439*).

This preacher Scervant Jones also owned the Swan Tavern in Yorktown in 1811.[134] Interestingly, the Swan Tavern was owned by **William Wills [Matt Wills?]** then perhaps came briefly into the possession of the heirs of **Wm Jones** In his 1824 (War. Co.) will[135] Wm Jones states:

> 'I appoint my friend **Servant Jones** and my son William my executors, to whom I give full power to Sell if necessary any part of my personal estate for the purpose of purchasing, or in other way to arrange or secure the Swan Tavern made over to me by Mr. Wills or to obtain the debt or money thereby secured, and in the event of their purchasing said property, it is my wish that it shall be by them sold again and the money arising from such sale of the property itself in their discretion ...'

Title to the Swan Tavern or lot seems to have passed somehow thru the hands of the **Nelsons, Rev. James Sclater** [in 1707], **Matt. Wills** [26 Dec 1781], **Lawrence Gibbons, Rev, Scervant Jones** [1811], _ **Wills, William Jones** ? [1824], and National Park Service.

Matt Jones II and Frances Servant had a son (the only known child of that m.) named Servant Jones. This first Servant Jones in our study is mentioned in his father's will of 1727/8[136] as a child and therefore would have been b. between 1708 and 1727. His earliest appearance in the existing Warwick Co. Court Records (2 Mar 1748) on a jury (/289) suggests that he would have been b. 1727 or before, agreeable to the calculated time frame.

We do not know how the guardianship of '**cozen Matthew**' and '**sister Marget**' was handled or who lived where after the 1727/8 w. of Matthew II, but we can be fairly sure that **Servant**, later aka 'Maj. SJ', lived in his MJH at least from the time of his 21st birthday and be quite sure that this Servant was the one who often appears in the surviving 18th century court records of Warwick County.

Servant was foreman on Grand Juries in 1756 (/428) & 1760 (/498), inspector at Denbeigh Warehouse 4 Jun 1761, in 1759 an Ensign and 6 Aug 1761 Lt. Col. of the 1st company of militia (/527), and in the same year recommended to the Commission of Peace.

---

[134] **Trudell, Clyde F.,** *Colonial Yorktown*, 1971 /99.

[135] Dunn:2018/72-3. Another preacher, James Sclater, bought Swan Tavern in 1707.

[136] The will of MJ II is in Isle of Wight Co. *Will bk 3*.

This **Servant Jones** was summoned to court 31 Dec 1770 with **Matthew Wood**, witnessed a w. 25 Oct 1773 *[Executive Journal VI/546]*, made his own w. 20 Nov 1772-- proved on 11 Feb 1773, all in Warwick Co.[137] It names chen **Allen, Mary, Matthew, William, James Servant, John, and gr'dau Frances**, dau of his deceased son **Phillip**. And he mentions a brother **Albridgton**. A wife is not mentioned. A somewhat disturbing clause says,

> By my deceased father's last Will and Testament the Reversion of several tracts or parcels of land will be my property at the death of my brother, Albridgton Jones, and when that shall happen my Will and desire is that my Executor shall bring suit against the person and all persons that shall have possession or claim the said lands, and if the said lands shall be recovered or any part thereof ...

A possible explanation is that according to the rule of *primogeniture*, which would continue until 1787 in VA, Servant Jones could *claim* the right of reversion and argue that the lands 'given' in his father's will were actually lifetime grants and not permanent property rights. His statement '*if* the said lands shall be recovered' is an indication that the reversion idea is debatable. However, it remains unprovable that *this* Matthew II was the father of *this* Servant, and I'm grateful to Mr. **Lyndon Hart** at LVA for his comments. Meanwhile s.a. *VA Land, M., & Pr. Recs, 1639-1850*, re Agatha and reversion to AJ.

The **William Servant Jones [Sr.]** whose will of 1824 names a son William i.e. **William Servant Jones [Jr.]** (3 Oct 1804-post 19 Apr 1866). There is confusion about these two men. Sr. mentions a wife in his will but does not name her; she is apparently a dau of **Carter Burwell**, she survives Wm, but is not named. One might suppose her to be the **Sarah C.** who witnessed the will, but Sarah C. was **Mrs. Allen** before she became **Sarah C. Jones**, so she must have been the wife of William S. Jones Jr. – a conclusion which not only leaves the wife of William S. Sr. unnamed in the 1824 will but also unnamed in the resulting probate action of the court.

Wm S., Jr. (3 Oct 1804-) m. (1) Mrs. **Sarah C[arpenter] Allen** and (2) 5 Mar 1830 **Mary Ann Wood** (w. 23 Aug 1862 pr. 12 Jul 1866).[138]–The chen were **Mary**

---

[137] Servant's w. is in Dunn:2016/19, and his est acct of 1782 is in Dunn:2019/1. The d. of SJ on 4 Feb 1773 is noted in *21W60* of Jul 1912 (citing the *VA Gazette*).

Francis (d. unm), **John Wood Jones** (dyng), **Jones, Sarah** (1832-) [she m. **William Crafford**; the chen of Sarah & William incl **Dr. John Crafford** m. **Eva Salter** (a descendant of whom is **Dr. Mercer Crafford** of Denbeigh)], **George** and **Henry Francis Jones** (1839-24 Jul 1920) who m. in 1866 **Justinia Newman**; their chen[139] were **Sue** c1867-), **William H.** (c1869-), **Harry** (c1871-), **Frank** (c1872-) and **Fannie** (1873-1976).[140] Fannie m. 1900 **John Turnley Wright.**[145] Fannie was b.27 Feb 1873, d. 15 Nov 1976. No Issue.

Rev. Scervant Jones (c1785-1854) was a rep of York Co. in the House of Delegates. He lived at King's Creek in 1827 and in Wmsbg in 1828, 1850,[146] & 1854.[147] His 3 letters to the citizens of York Co. at the VA Hist. Society date from 4 Mar 1824 when they apparently were published in Richmond. He relates some of the actions of the Legislature as well as his own thoughts. He says, solitary confinement is 'the very refinement of cruelty itself,' and 'I should delight to see capital punishment stricken from our code,' and 'In old VA industry and economy were considered the only sure means of acquiring wealth, we were then prosperous and happy. In an evil hour the tempter came—banks were established and soon after idleness, extravagance and luxury were seen through our land.' About slavery he wrote, 'The time has arrived when we ought to lay the axe to the root of this great evil.'

York Deeds 8/439 show a deed dated 26 Dec 1817 from **SJ & Nancy Timson,** his wife; signed Nancy T. Jones. On the next page she is noted as **Ann Timson Jones.**

York Order Bk 1829-35 **SJ & Nancy T.,** his wife mention 17 Jan 1831

An interesting membership application (to Sons of the American Revolution) re **Matthew Wood** (20 Nov 1757 - 21 Oct 1839,) *from* War. Co. (and mentioned in War. Co. crt recs from 1770):

---

[139] *Fedcen for 1880*   [Fn 138 not in use]
[140] *Times-Herald of NN 16 Nov 1976* and *Col. Ridgell's c1965 interview with Fannie*
(footnotes 141-144 not in use)
[145] *Soldier, Veteran & Prisoner Rolls & Lists [Ancestor.com]*
[146] In 1828 he signed a pet. to change the line betw. York & James City Counties [in *York Co. Petitions 1805-1839*]; in 1850 he was in the fedcen for Williamsburg.
[147] Rev, Scervant Jones was bu. in Wmsbg in 1854 *[Find A Grave].* Rockefeller Lib. in Wmsbg has letters and sermons by him.

Allen Dudley Jones, lawyer, gives his b. as 2 Nov 1876 at Yorktown, a resident of ECC, with an address in NN.[149] He was son of **John Sheldon Jones** b. 1 May 1841 in York, d. 12 Oct 1921 and **Jamie [or Jennie?] Eagle Jones** b. in Kent Co. MD. 27 Dec 1848, d. ECC, VA, 24 Jun 1925, m. in York Co. 1871. He was grandson of **John Allen Jones** b. in York Co. 2 Nov 180[8?], d. 3 May 1885[150] and **Elizabeth Wynne Jones** b.1811 in Warwick, d. in York in 1841, m. in York 1827.

He was gr-grson of **Servant Jones**[146] b. 4 Aug 1789 in York or Warwick, d. 30 Dec 1808 in York, and **Margaret Wood Jones** b. 25 Nov 1790 in Warwick Co., d. 10 Feb 1852 in York or Warwick, m. 1807. ADJ was the gr-gr gr'son of **Matthew Wood** b. 20 Dec 1757 in Warwick Co., d. 21 Oct 1839 in York, m. **Margaret Moss Wood** in 1786; she b. 10 Feb 1762 in York, d. 18 Jan 1837. **Matthew Wood** enlisted 1775 in 1st VA Regiment under **Cpt. Thomas Nelson**.

Graphical :

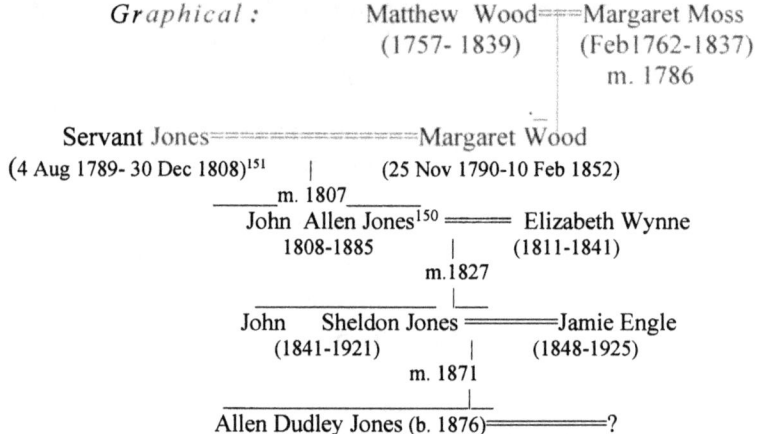

Related or Unrelated (and miscellaneous)

Apparent errors should be noted: In *6T47* is the name 'Nancy Simpson Buckner', supposedly b. in 1800, wife of **Rev Scervant Jones**, but that seems to be a confusion of names. Correct is 'Anne [Nancy] Timson Buckner' (Ann

---

[149] A.D. Jones is mentioned also in *9T137*.
[150] A **John Allen Jones** (d. 1844) was the son of **Kim. Jones & Mary P. Hogan** (*NJ Bible 1758-1915*); this same source shows a John Allen Jones (same prnts) b. 1833. Mary P. Hogan m. 10 May 1821 (Bible of NJ 1758-1915).
[151] This SJ was not found in existing records. The shortness of his life might have contributed to the lack of records.

was b. in 1787). The same source indicates a sale of Swan Tavern by the said Servant & Nancy in 1781, and that is also wrong; the date digits were transposed (from 1817).

Misc Servant Jones (c1782 - 7 Jun 1863); another (c1860 - 26 Feb 1860); both d. in Charleston, SC [SC Death Records, 1821-1965]

LVA, Bernard J. Henley Papers /2-3: "Cpt Servant Jones [d.] a good magistrate & impartial inspector of tob." [from newspaper]

I've seen records, of a **Servant Jones** in Australia and on a passenger list to UK in the 1860s – 1880s, and another in SC c1863 (b. c1782); for these I can only imagine that they were other descendants of Bertrand Servant or his parents.

Bertie a record in Bertie Co., NC, is a bond from **Servant** (signed 'Sarven[t]') Jones on the m. to **Temperance Taylor** 12 Jan 1782;[152]

Chatham and **Halifax** *NC Rev. War Pay Vouchers, 1779-1782* show SJs in mil. Service in Halifax and Chatham Cos.

James Servant Jones witnessed the sale of a slave 21 Nov 1787 ['miscellaneous' section, *'Slave and Free Persons of Color' Records of Chatham Co., NC., NC State Archives*].

ECC One SJ d. 24 Sep 1896 in ECC

IoW one d. 7 Feb 1772 in IoW [McSwain /223 citing VA Gazette.]. *9T280* SJ records 1736 IoW Co., VA. Newman: "Prob nr the time when he was 21." **'cozen Matthew'** m. **Martha Harwood**

Meck... W. of TJ 1802 *[9T137]*

No'ton Co., NC Servant Jones d. bef 25 May 1825. *Northampton Co.,*

The *1790 fedcen* for Nor'ton lists an SJ.

SJ was listed in the *1790 fedcen* for Northampton, NC, in the 1830 fedcen for York Co., and in the fedcen for Wmsbg for 1850 (showing his b. at c1785).

---

[152] *NC M. Records 1741-2011*

The land of a 'Servent' Jones (- bef. 5 Mar 1825) was to be divided in a pet. of 25 May 1825 in Nor'ton Co., NC. **James Jones** 21, & bro of **Robt** were sons. [*NC Estate Files*]

LDS lists an SJ in 1809 in Nor'ton Co., NC

Portsmouth   An SJ d. 18 Jan 1887 in Portsmouth, VA

Wake   **James Servant Jones** 1805 in Orange Co., NC

Williamsbg and **Warwick**   A grandson of **Frances Servant**, **John Sr.** m. **Mary Hubbard** and had several chen incl John Jr's sons (incl **William Servant Jones**)

1850 fedcen for Wmsbg showing SJ's b. c1785

VA Colonial Soldiers 6 Aug 1761 SJ Lt of 1st Company

The *colonial court* mentions of SJ from 1748 to 1770 incl pp 289, 331, 370, 428, 498, 507, 523, and 527.
4
The *1850 fedcen* for Williamsburg shows a '**Fannie I**', age 38, in the household of SJ. Presumably Fannie was helping out after the death of **Ann** on 6 Jun 1849.[153] In that same report is named **William B.**, nephew of **Rev. Scervant Jones,** The other names listed there, **Roper and Pollard,** are unknown to this researcher.

6T47: Rev. Scervant Jones m. (1) Ann Timson Buckner, (2) **Mrs. Pollard** (? -RD)

York A SJ was of age by 27 Feb 1804 [b. c1785?]   [*6T47*]

York Orders   1820 mention

York Orders   c1820 **SJ & Nancy**

York Orders 1820-1825   SJ ex for **JJ**? 16 Nov 1824

---

[153] *LDS-Pedigree Resource File*. And the *1850 fedcen*. Ann was b. 1 Sep 1787, so she was abt. 1 ½ yrs younger than her husband whom she m. at age 18 (on 26 Dec 1805).

York Order Bk 12, 1829-1835/90   SJ gdn of **Mary & Hinde** 21 Mar 1831

York Jdmts & Ords 1759-1763/435   **SJ Sr** suit 20 Sep 1762

York Jdmts & Ords 1768-70/84   15 Aug 1768

6T48: **Allen Jones** of Yorktown   grantee 10 Oct 1783   cites York recs

York Deeds 8/439 SJ & **Nancy T.** grantors   to Matthew Wills 16 Jun 1817

York Deeds 8/130 rel. to **Thos. Tabb** 21 Jan 1811

York Deeds SJ date of last entry wi Nancy T. 16 Mar 1842

York Deeds   date of last entry for SJ 12 Apr 1854

An SJ named in the *1830 fedcen* for York Co., VA.

A SJ resided in York Co. in 1840 [*1840 fedcen*].

17 Sep 1828 a petition[154] regarding York Co. and James City Co. borders he d. c1805 in NC[155]

An SJ d. 25 Nov 1787 [*Hustings Crt.*]

York M. Bonds & Consents   **John A. Jones** m. **Eliz Wynne** 3 Jun 1827

York Order Bk4 (1774-84) /167   TJ ex for **HJ** 20 Jul 1778

York Deeds SJ date of last entry wi Nancy T. 16 Mar 1842

York Deeds   date of last entry for SJ 12 Apr 1854

An SJ named in the *1830 fedcen* for York Co., VA.

A SJ resided in York Co. in 1840 [*1840 fedcen*].

An SJ d. 25 Nov 1787 [*Hustings Crt.*]

---

[154] *York Co. Petitions 1805-1839.*
[155] *NC Wills and Probate Records, 1665-1998*

York M. Bonds & Consents   **John A. Jones m. Eliz Wynne** 3 Jun 1827

***

This part looks like this:

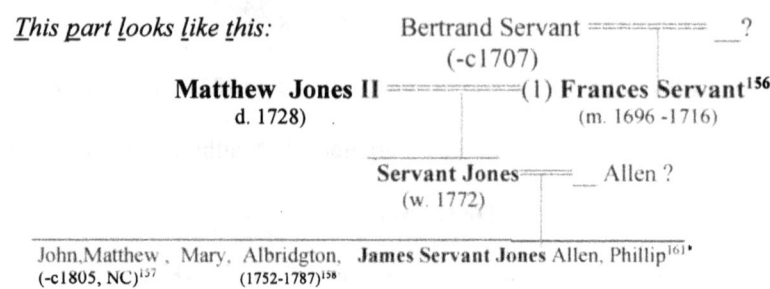

```
                          Bertrand Servant ═══════ ?
                              (-c1707)
           Matthew Jones II ═══════(1) Frances Servant[156]
              d. 1728)                  (m. 1696 -1716)

                        Servant Jones ═══ Allen ?
                          (w. 1772)

John,Matthew, Mary, Albridgton,  James Servant Jones Allen, Phillip[161]*
  (-c1805, NC)[157]       (1752-1787)[158]
```

York Orders   c1820   **SJ & Nancy**

York Orders 1820-1825   SJ ex for **JJ**? 16 Nov 1824

York Order Bk 12, 1829-1835/90   SJ gdn of **Mary & Hinde** 21 Mar 1831

York Jdmts & Ords 1759-1763/435   **SJ Sr** suit 20 Sep 1762

York Jdmts & Ords 1768-70/84   15 Aug 1768

6T48: **Allen Jones** of Yorktown   grantee 10 Oct 1783   cites York recs

York Deeds 8/439   SJ & **Nancy T**. grantors   to Matthew Wills 16 Jun 1817

---

[156] The 1st **Frances Servant Jones** is not the dau of **Phillip**, the granddau mentioned in the 1772 w. of **Servant Jones**, who m. **John Pate Wills**, was b. in 1770 and became a ward of **Allen Jones** on 14 Aug 1777; presumably her mother was her first guardian and presumably her mother d. c1777. She (the dau of Phillip) sued for her share of her grandfather's estate.
[157] *NC Wills and Probate Records*
[158] A curiosity of this w. is that it was recorded in York Co. (Hustings Court 1787-1795, pps 1-3, turning the book upside-down and reading from the back) even though he stated that he lived at Bourbon in the parish and county of Warwick. An explanation is that the enabling act for the incorporation of Yorktown provided that freeholders having a residence there at the time of death were entitled to full rights. Allen owned 92 acres there and thus would be a legal resident (*General Index to Deeds 1777-1956,* /415).

York Deeds 8/130 rel. to **Thos. Tabb** 21 Jan 1811

York Deeds SJ date of last entry wi Nancy T.16 Mar 1842

York Deeds date of last entry for SJ 12 Apr 1854

An SJ named in the *1830 fedcen* for York Co., VA.

A SJ resided in York Co. in 1840 [*1840 fedcen*].

17 Sep 1828 a petition[159] regarding York Co. and James City Co. borders he d. c1805 in NC[160]

An SJ d. 25 Nov 1787 [*Hustings Crt.*]

Y*ork M. Bonds & Consents* **John A. Jones** m. **Eliz Wynne** 3 Jun 1827.

York Order Bk4 *(1774-84) /167* TJ ex for **HJ** 20 Jul 1778

```
    JJ Sr═══ Sarah Hubbard¹⁶¹              Mary Tabb
    ─────┬──                               ─────┬──
   John Jones, Jr ═╤═(1) Sarah Duncan in 1803    Mary    Bourbon
   (b. 1779)       │                             m. (2) ___ ?
   Wm Servant Jones═╤═(1)Sarah C. Allen          ─────┬──
   (1804 - 12 Jul 1866) │                        Allen    Nancy
         William Benjamin Jones¹⁶²                m. (3) Lucy Moss
   ──────┬────────────
```

---

[159] *York Co. Petitions 1805-1839.*
[160] *NC Wills and Probate Records, 1665-1998*
[161] McS gives the first name of **Miss Hubbard** as **Sarah** (her p. 223), citing an article by **Mary Hubbard** in *7T134- 6* and *9T281* (who cited a family Bible). She gives the chen of John and Sarah Hubbard as: Sarah, 3 unnamed daus, John Jr., and Scervant (Jones). She also names the chen of **John Jones, Jr.** and his wife **Sarah Duncan,** as **Francis M.** (b. 1806) and **Bourbon Jones.** Another **William** m. **Mary Duncan** (15 Mar 1776-1826) in VA in Nov 1819.
[162] He was the son of the 1ˢᵗ m. of **William S. Jones (to Mrs. Sarah Carpenter Allen).** S.a. *DAR Bible recs v. 55, Series 2* re **'Hellcat' Billy**. But in *6T46* his fa was JJ Sr. and his mother M̶a̶r̶y̶ [Sarah] Hubbard.

(2) MaryAnn Wood Lucy[163] Servant
(3 Oct 1804-post 19 Apr 1866)[164] (d. 4 Feb 1773)
m.5 May 1830

The chen of the 2nd m. of **William S[ervant] Jones** (to **Mary Ann Wood**) were **Sarah** (1832-), John Wood (Jones) (dyng), **Mary Frances** (dsp) and **Henry Francis Jones** (1839-1920). From the 3rd m., **Lucy** m. 29 Sep 1801 **Matthew Wills** *[6 T146]*. Both were 21.

An estate sale of a '**Capt. Servient Jones**' was on 11 Jul 1782; the witnesses included **Allen Jones** and **Robert Lucas**. This Servient could not have been the son of **Allen** and **Lucy Moss**, a child of perhaps nine or ten in 1782. This man was also not the **Servant Jones** whose w. was proved in 1773.

Vinkler

This is another name that we encounter often in this study. Vinkler Sr's prnts were **MJ & Mary Lee**.~~168~~ He was b. c1749[165]; his will dated 5 Sep 1817 was recorded Sep 1831 in [Granville Co., NC, in *Bk 12/229 & pp 1136-7]*, and names wife **Elizabeth [Armistead]**[166] and chen **Mary T. Jones** (c1766-c1827) who m. **Robert Harris, Westwood Armistead Jones** (c1771-c1829) who m. **Delilah Jones** [their dau **Eliz.** [aka **Betsy**] **N. Leathers**], **John Jones** (c1776-aft 1820) who m. **Judith Booth** [their chen **Sintha & George**], **Francis Jones** (c1778-aft 1819) who m. **Nancy Booth**, **William Westwood Jones** (c1771-c1829) m. **Eliz. Norman, Nancy Harwood Jones** who m. **Harper Booth, Eliz. Jones** (c1780-aft 1817) m. **Burrow**, and **Vinkler Jones, Jr.** (c1775-aft 1817).[167]

Tom Krakow writes about Vinkler Jones [in *7JHA2 (Spring 2001) /2*] that he was b. c1744 (calculated from 1756 land ownership) and that he was prob b. in VA. The name appears in the 1764 lists of tithables for Luneburg Co., VA near **TJ Sr & Jr, HJ** and other Joneses [He (Tom) doesn't cite sources]. It is generally agreed that Vinkler m. **Eliz. Armistead**, dau of Sr. and **Mary Tabb**. He appears several times in Meck'l Co. deeds from 1766-1768. Abt 1768 he moved to Granville Co., NC when he bought land there Jul 1768, and appears in the 1769 tax lists for Granville Co., in the Granville militia in

---

[163] **Lucy Moss** and **Allen Jones** had a son Servant Jones (or '**Serviento**.')
[164] McS cites **Vollertson**, *Who was Who*, Ft. Eustis Historical & Archaeological Assn for the birth date.
[165] *Rootsweb*
[166] *6T128*: she was his sis-in-law. *6T130:* she m. John Armistead.
[167] The estimated dates were provided by **Barry Hayes** in *7JHA2*/2 (Spring 2001).

1771, and property recs in later documents. In his w. he transfers property to his sons, daus & grchen. Vinkler Sr. d. c1818. [We do not know which recs pertain to Vinkler Sr and which, if any, to Jr.]

Related or Unrelated

Misc *fedcen 1810*/136   Jones, Jr., Vinkler   Grv 887

6Tyler128-131   Jones, Vinkler (bro of **John Armstead**'s wife)   m, **Elizabeth Armstead**. She was dau of **Westwood Armistead & Mary Tabb**. Eliz Armistead was his sis-in-law; cites "*Quarterly vol. 7*, p 20"

11T34: Mary was dau of **Col. John Tabb**.   **Wm Jones** [son of Vinkler, W 1817]   M. 1808   Oxford, NC.   date printed: 1908. Son **T.P.Eppes Armistead Jones** M 10 Jun 1835 **Mary Frances Hawkins**; their chen: **William, Westwood** et al.   Westwood m. Eliz. Johnson, **Mary M** (1) Mr Foster, (2) John Burnell, Lucy m. Richd Harris, Betty, John Armistead, Thos, Norma.

NC Rev. Pay Vouchers show Vinkler for 25 Feb 1781.

US, WW I Draft Reg, Cards, 1917-18 list **Vinkler Robert Jones** b. 10 Jun 1878, residing in Bastrop, TX. The *US Find a Grave Index* gives his b. as 1878 and d. as 1938.

Ecc   *6T128-131*   Jones, Vinkler (bro of John Armstead's wife) m. Eliz Armstead, dau of Westwood Armistead & Mary Tabb. Also *11T34*. Mary was dau of Col. John Tabb.

6T128:   Jones, Vinkler *court rec of 7 Oct 1766*: wife recovered interest in est of her fa.   wife: Elizabeth (b. between Jul 1721 and Jul 1722); fa-in-l: Westwood; mo-in-law: Mary Tabb. Col. John Tabb lived nearby. His bros **Tingnall, Harwood** lived in Granville Co.(1790 in Northam., NC). Lydia's w. pr 28 Oct 1773 in Hampton; her sons   (bros?): **Tingnal, Harwood, Francis, John,Vinkler; siss: Margaret Thompsn, Elisa. Armistead**

Franklin   NC *Est Files* for Franklin Co.—45 pps—(records involve Granville Co. also) His bros were **John, FJ, Wm**, sis **Margaret Booth**. FJ was ex. for Vinkler [Jr] (d. in 1817) 5 Mar 1818. **Vinkler Sr**. made deposition re disputed will of his son 23 Apr 1818. Mentions **Louisa Maria Jones, Elizabeth, Caroline Jones, Westwood, Vinkler** et al.

Granville *6T128*   Jones, Vinkler [Sr] & **Eliz.**   judgmnt for 7 Oct 1766 Eliz City Co.   interest in estate of Westwood [Armistead]; her fa's Bros: Tingnall, Harwood   he & Ting. lived in Granville Co. (in Northam., NC in 1790).   Vinkler is in *1790 fedcen* for Granville Co, Sr

11T34+   Jones, Vinkler. *cites Bk 12/229*   W. rec   Sep 1831 Granville Co., NC.   d 5 Sep 1817   wife: Eliz.; sons: **Westwood A.**, **John**, **(his son Vinkler), Francis, Wm;** daus **Mary Harris, Nancy Booth, Eliz. Burrow.**

Hampton *6T128+*   **Jones, Lydia**   W. pr 28 Oct 1773 Hampton   sons: Tingnal (Tignal), Harwood, Francis, John, Vinkler; Sisters Marg.Thompson, Eliz.Armistead; info on ncs, cns

Meck W. pr   13 Oct 1794   *[6T45]* wife Martha

Wake   Jones, Tignal   W.   25 Sep 1849   Wake Co., NC wife: Emiline M. Jones; sons: Vinkler R. & John P.

Bentley:1983 /162   Jones, Vinkler   m.   24 Nov 1823   Wake Co., NC   Euny Rogers

Some of the entries not mentioned elsewhere are in *NC Estate Files* for <u>Wake</u> Co.: 1) '**Vinclair** *(1824)*' his wife **Unice** (sp?). '**Vinkler' Jones.**   His dau **Ann V. Jones** m. **Douglas F. Hodges** 25 Dec 1839; Douglas reached 21 on 23 Dec 1841 and thus was b. 23 Dec 1820.

In *NC Est Files* for Wake: 18 pps: Pet [re land partition] by **TJ, FJ, Richd Smith** & wife **Penny** <u>vs</u> **Betsy Leathers,** widow of **William Leathers, James Newbern** & wife **Martha, William Allen** & wife **Ann, Thos H. Scasborough** & wife **Mary, Augustus Hunter** & wife **Maria, James A. Waddell** & wife **Margaret, Douglas Hodges** & wife **Ann V.** ... [Petitioners] are the chen and grch of **Westwood & Deliah,** both dec'd. The land was conveyed by TJ, dec'd, by deed of trust to **Redding,** dec'd ... Ann V. and **Martha C.** not of age.... All the dfts reside in TN; names **Jack Mariah Jones and Francis A.** Mentions tripartite indenture 26 Aug 1807 of **Col. TJ Sr, Redding & John C.** Jones. Delilah was dau of TJ. [There is confusion about Louisa Maria or Mariah Jones

Briggs and Joneses

Charles Briggs esq., son of a Rev War soldier,[168] was not only husband (the first husband) of **Elizabeth Jones** but was in close association with many of the NC Joneses. In 1792 **Charles** had a lot next to **Tignal Jones** (lots 184 & 185 on Hillsboro Street in Raleigh)[169] and near the two lots of **Nathaniel(s)** (131 & 276).[170] Earlier (1719) he or another Charles Briggs was involved in a lnd deed in IoW.[171] In these times (1780s to at least Dec 1794) his name appears in the court records for Wake County showing him on committees with **Redding, Tignal Sr. & Jr., and Nathaniel Sr. & Jr.** (*Bk II/108, III/13+54+61*). The Sept term 1794 of Wake County records[172] shows many of them: e.g. 'Ordered that **TJ Sr, NJ (WP), NJ (CT), NJ sr, and Charles Briggs**...divide ...the Estate of **JJ** dec'd ... amongst the orphans of JJ ...'

Charles began a gradual decline in health c1798. In Mar 1798 wife **Betsy** was ordered by the court of Wake County to give in a list of the taxable property of **Charles Briggs**, in case of his refusal to do it himself. On the following Mar the court did a formal inquiry into the condition of **Charles Briggs**, and on 18 Dec 1800 he was declared a 'lunatick'[173]-- in all probability a term indicating some unspecified inability on his part to handle his personal affairs properly. Elizabeth's father, **Col. Tingnal Jones, Sr.**, well-known to the Court as justice, was appointed guardian of him and his estate.

Tingnall moved to be discharged from the guardianship in Feb 1801. Charles died intestate not long after, as the court minutes of Aug 1801 mention him as deceased. Tingnall,Sr. was appointed administrator. A preliminary view of the estate was ordered in Aug 1801 and an estate sale was set in Feb 1802. Meanwhile a committee was appointed 10 Sep 1801 to allot an allowance to

---

[168] *The Colonial & State Records of NC* 17/197 shows that he received pay voucher 3008 from **Nathaniel Williams.** S.a. *NC State Archives, Treasurer and Comptroller Records, Military Papers, vols 40-66; Index to Revolutionary Army Accounts IV/42 Folio 2; Bk of Settlements No. 28 [vol 52]/15; Receipt Bk [vol 54] /231; Index to Misc. Volumes, Bk 19 [vol 51] /34.* Charles Briggs, probably the father of this Charles Briggs, patented 225 acres in Surry Co VA 16 Jun 1714 (*LVA Land Records* /170-171).
[169] 1792 *Plan of the City of Raleigh.*
[170] We do not know who these Nathaniels were.
[171] *Grimes:1980* /217
[172] *NC Estate Files for Wake Co.* under JJ (1803)
[173] The bond for the 'lunacy' of Charles Briggs is in the NC State Archives. The instrument also bound Tignal Jones' sons Redding and Fanning.

Elizabeth (*Wake Co. W Bk 5/337*; s.a. Wynne, *Wake Co NC Abstracts of Wills 1771-1802*).

The Jones-Alston Connection

Mrs. Elizabeth (Jones) Briggs === Absalom Alston
(- c1839)   (- 1828)
c1803

Duncan D.   Elizabeth   Calvin J.   Christian   Mary Stuart = David Harding
(1808-)   (prob dii)   (1813-1835)   (c1806-)
           1829 =|== Pleasant Wright
                     (c1807-)

Harwood Jones

Harwood III belongs to the generation of grandson to **Matthew [I] and Elizabeth Albridgeton** and we will take up his parentage shortly. First let's consider the man himself. He was b. c1728 or before if we assume that he was at least 21 when he served on a grand jury 6 Apr 1749 (/289). During the ensuing years we know that he was mentioned very frequently in existing fragments of court records as estate examiner or appraiser, as Justice of the Peace, administrator, guardian, on the Commission of Peace, supplying bonds for security, and so forth. It was especially during the years 1755 to 1761 that he was active on the court of Warwick Co. He became Captain of militia on 2 Jul 1761 (/525) and just a month later – on 6 Aug 1761 (/526) became sheriff for the county. He d. 1771 *[6T146]*

Guardianship   Harwood Jones had been guardian for **Tignal Jones,** 'orph. of Matthew' (/514 1 Jan 1761, & /527 6 Aug 1761), but no record exists to tell us when that Matthew died or when the guardianship began. But it had nevertheless practically ended—because Harwood selected Tignal as under-Sheriff (for War. Co.) in the session of 6 Aug 1761. This Tignal was probably a cousin and evidently the guardianship ended in 1761, the same court session as the presumably final guardianship accounting for Tignal (also / 527)}. That would put the b. of this Tignal at c1740 and put the b. of his (Tignal's) father, **Matthew**, at around 1720.

Harwood Jones was also chosen guardian by **Judith Jones** (/469 7 Sep 1758), probably his sister. Two years earlier (/437, 7 Oct 1756), Harwood Jones had secured court authorization for the administration of his mother **Martha's** estate; that indicates that her husband had d., and we can further presume that

Martha was the first guardian of Judith and her other chen, of whom Judith could have been the only minor. That suggests a b. year for Judith at around late 1730's. Harwood Jones was also guardian to other chen including **Frances Jones** (/461 6 Apr 1758), dau of **John Jones**. She later m. **James Southall**. This action was secured by the bond of another Francis Jones – not his father.

Militia, Marriage & Death, Parentage He served in the militia under **Lt. Harwood Jones** [*County Militia Rosters, Virginia's Colonial Soldiers /36*].

Harwood Jones m. **Mary Chisman** in 1744[174]. He lived in the upper precincts of Warwick Co. (/394 1755), perhaps near to the **John Joneses** who provided security for his acts of administration or guardianship. He d. 9 Feb 1771.[175]

Re the parentage of Harwood Jones: McSwain is probably correct in placing him as the son of **Matthew Jones** who m. **Martha Harwood,** the grandson of **Francis Jones** who m. **Mary Tingnall** (her p. 184) *[IoW deeds 5 Jun 1760 re 250 a. from MJ & Mary, his wife, of York Co. to Jas. Watson, which anciently belonged to Matthew Jones the Elder and was given to his sons Matt. and Francis, since...FJ sold his part to Matt; this Matthew lived in York Co. where his w. of 10 Aug 1762 was proved 15 Nov 1762. It is too mutilated but mentions Matthew Jones and directs that a house be built for her in Martin's Hundred]. [HJ produced his acct agst Tingnall Jones, orph of Matthew Jones (XIII WM143)]*[176]

An HJ m. **Eliz. Jarrell** in *So'ton Co., VA M. Bk. /4*; the w. is in *No'ton Co., NC WB 1/484 (1789-)*. {Associated wi 1798 w. of HJ Jr. [*No'ton WB 2/169 (1798)*]} HJ m. Eliz. Jarrell 4 Oct 1758. [*Select Ms.1785-1940*]

McSwain is probably correct in naming **Judith, Francis, and Harwood** as chen of **Matthew Jones & Martha Harwood**, probably correct in placing the **Francis Jones** who m. **Mary Ridley** as a son of the Francis who m. Miss Tingnall.

---

[174] According to CWD. But CWD is mixed up on other details about Harwood Jones: his b. year, siblings, father's dates. (See p.50 in Dunn:2019*)*
[175] A record is in 13*WM70.*
[176] From *6T45*

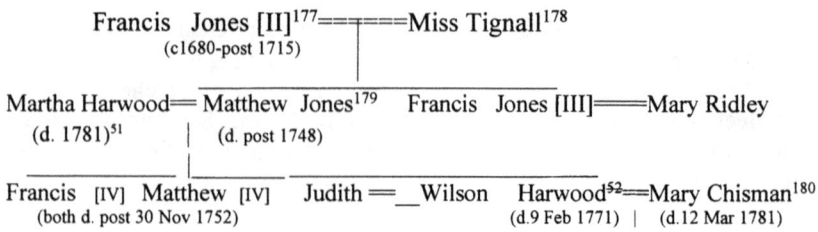

Francis Jones [II][177]====Miss Tignall[178]
(c1680-post 1715)

Martha Harwood==Matthew Jones[179]   Francis Jones [III]====Mary Ridley
(d. 1781)[51]   (d. post 1748)

Francis [IV] Matthew [IV]   Judith ==_Wilson Harwood[52]==Mary Chisman[180]
(both d. post 30 Nov 1752)   (d.9 Feb 1771) | (d.12 Mar 1781)

McSwain goes on to provide evidence for the placement of the brothers **Matthew & Francis** as sons of Matthew & Martha Harwood (quoting from her pps 184-187). For additional sources see *York Co. Records of 20 Jul 1778 [IV/167 & 174]*, and *McIlvaine VI/546*.

Related or Unrelated

Misc. *Wilson Library, U of NC, NC Collection /72*   HJ m. Eliz

NC Estate Files – Franklin and Granville Cos. (45 pps) p.8 orphs of Harwood Jones were **John & Henry** – 1823.
OR: HJ d. intestate in Halifax in 1816; wife **Eliz.**, orphs **John & Henry**

HJ (7 Sep 1775 in Meck'l Co., VA, - 23 Feb 1837 in Marion, Perry Co. AL). Wife, **Rachel M.**; chen **Julia Rachel Bates, William E., Oscar M., Mary Frances Jones, Martha A. Jones, Lucy Maria Jones, Susan J. Jones,** infant dau, & **Eliz. Ann Sanders Lowry.** This may be the same **HJ** who m. **Rachel Crenshaw** 20 Oct 1809 in Meck'l Co. [*VA Compiled Ms, 1740-1850*].

---

[177] '[II]' = the generation of the *chen* of **Matthew Jones** and **Eliz. Albridgeton.** Subsequent generations are [III], [IV], etc. in my numbering system. McSwain uses a somewhat different numbering system. By my numbering, e.g. Matthew II is the son of Matthew I who m. Eliz Albridgeton, and likewise Francis II is of the same generation as Matt II.

[178] McSwain cites *English Duplicates...* /29; (her p.183)

[179] *Dunn:2008* /65

[180] *Chisman Bible (1682-1781)*; s.a. York Co. records 20 Jul 1778 (IV/167 & 174 as well as *13W1/70*. Probably Mary was the dau of **Wm. Harwood Chisman** witnessed his w. [1752], but there was another Mary Chisman—the wife of **John Chisman** (/357). We note that Wm. Chisman and Harwood Jones were on the court together for at least the years 1750-1761, and Mary Chisman had witnessed a w. in 1752 for which estate Wm Harwood was named an executor (/364).

HJ (Heywood Jones) (15 May 1834 - 5 May 1858). **Martha Jones** (22 Apr 1834, 22 Aug 1908). – Both bu. at Jones Cemetery, 11 mi E of Angier, NC. [*Hist. Recs. Survey of NC*]

6Tyler45: Jones, Harwood [*Eliz City Co. Rec. 23 Feb 1768*]. Justice of Warwick Co.,VA & Cpt. of militia. W. not preserved. exs apparently **Wm. Harwood & Tignal Jones**

York Jdmts & Ords 1768-70/124, 201 HJ suit 20 Jun 1768

HJ m. 2 Oct 1744 **Mary Chisman**, wife **Matthew & Martha Jones**; prnts *Chisman Bible*: he d. 9 Feb 1771; Mary d. 12 Mar 1781 @age 51 *13W70*

HJ *9Tyler282* HJ d. 9 Feb 1771. Bro **Tingnall**; ward: Tingnall, orphan of Matt.' (neph). no issue; his bro was an ex of his w.

Elliot, *M. Recs...74* **Jones, Harwood Maj.** W. 24 Oct 1809 Meckl. Co., VA m. bond to **Rachel Crenshaw** 20 Oct 09. consent: **Thomas A, Jones,** gdn of Rachel;

York #3 Jdmts & Ords 1759-63 **Eleanor Chisman** to pay HJ for 10 mi.

ECC recs 23 Feb 1768 HJ justice & Cpt of militia [*6T45*] no w.

JCC *Fleet, ser 2, IV/36-7* land 23 Apr 1761. Wife Mary

Tingnal/Tignal Jones

The existing colonial court records for Warwick County show entries for Tignal (Tingnall) Jones for only the 5 years and 1 mo. 1 Jul 1756- 6 Aug 1761. A Tingnal, however, reportedly was b. in 1746[181] to **MJ** and his wife Mary Lee. Apparently upon reaching the age of majority he moved to Mecklenburg Co, VA, where he made a bond 16 Nov 1767 for the m. to **Sarah Anderson** (*VA, County m. Records, 1771-1943*).

One Tignal was involved in numerous civil functions for his county and country, as the colonial and *state recs of NC, the minutes of the Wake Co. Court,* and other documents show. The *DAR applications* prepared for **Mary Louise Phillips** and **Lydia Phillips** state that he was Delegate to the

---

[181] *DAR Ancestor #: A062750*, officer with the Mecklenburg County Militia. His birth date is listed as 1746.

provincial Congress, Member of Provincial Councils and Committee of Safety, member of the Provincial Council which met at Halifax, NC, 4 Apr 1776, delegate to a Congress of the Council of Safety 12 Nov 1776 at Halifax, Lt. Col of the Wake Co. Regiment of NC Militia 24 Apr 1776 [1778 in the DAR apl. of Mary Louise]; member of the NC Congress at Hillsborough Aug 1775; J.P. of Wake Co. Crt of Pleas and Quarter Session Dec 1776 throughout the war; represented Wake Co. in NC House of Commons in 1777, and a member of NC Provincial Congress at New Bern Apr 1775. Sources cited are: Wheeler's *History* I/77-8 and I/84-6; *Colonial Recs of NC IX*/1179, X/166, 501, 915; State Recs of NC XII/337, 600, 714, XXIII/995, and the family Bibles of **Willis G. Briggs** and **Kitura Briggs Harrington** (not in public use).

Tingnal and his brother Nathaniel served in the Wake Co. Militia as lt. and Capt., respectively, and are named in lists (in *NC Dept. of Archives and History*) of Oct 1772 and again of 6 Oct 1773, under the command of Col. Elliot, *M. Recs...74* **Jones, Harwood Maj.**   W. 24 Oct 1809   Meckl. Co., VA   m. bond to **Rachel Crenshaw** 20 Oct 09.   consent: **Thomas A, Jones,** gdn of Rachel;

York #3 Jdmts & Ords 1759-63 **Eleanor Chisman** to pay HJ for 10 mi.

HJ   *9Tyler282*   HJ d. 9 Feb 1771.   Bro Tingnall; ward: Tingnall, orphan of Matt.' (neph).   "no issue"; his bro was an ex of his w.

ECC recs 23 Feb 1768   HJ justice & Cpt of militia [*6T45*] no w.

JCC   *Fleet, ser 2, IV/36-7*

The nine chen of **Tingnal**[182] **Jones** (-- c1807), son of FJ & Mary Ridley, m. **Penelope Cain**[183] (d. aft 12 May 1813). Their chen were: [birth order unknown]. [*Wake Co. Bk7 /295+*] = W. rec Nov 1807]

1. **Francis** m. **Agnes Thompson** b. 1767 [*US and Interrnat'l M. Recs, 1560-1900*] 9 Jan 1789 in NC [Anon], d. 1844.
2. **Redding** (d. 1816)[184] m. **Martha Bustian Grant** [Anon], d. 1815 (w. pr. 1816). Chen: **John Ridley Jones** (who m. **Martha Lane**)[185]. She (Martha Bustian) had 1 son, **James Grant**, the fa of **Judge Grant**; James Grant m. a **Miss Whitaker**. [AAW says 'Miss Bustian m.—Ransome and had **Matthew Ransome**, and that **Patsy (Redding's)** chen were **Mary, Sarah, Thos, TJ, John,** and **Fanning**]. The *Pedigree Resource File* shows FJ's m. as c1804, his b. c1760, chen as **TJ, Fanning M. Jones, Thomas Jones, Sally Jones, Martha Jones** and **Mary Jones,** his fa as **Colonel TJ.**
   Notes by AAW: **Mary** m. **Calvin Nicholson, Sarah** m. **Dr. Murphy. Judge Spier Whitaker** is the nephew of Mrs. Grant,
3. **Fanning**[186] m. (l) **Mary Bustian** 1794, sister of brother Redding's wife Martha. m. (2) **Nancy Jeffreys** 25 Jun 1799 (*Wake Co. M. Bonds /263* also shows a m. to **Betsy Penny** *19 Nov 1829*). [AAW adds that Fanning had 2 sons, **David &** Fanning, but doesn't say wife 1 or 2.
4. **Tingnall, Jr.** (1766-1807) m. **Peggy Jeffreys** *[DAC, op. cit.]*, (Penny was widow).[185-6] Chen (per *NC Estate Files*)[186]: **TJ, Simon Jones, Willis**

---

[182] Tignal name: The 'importation' in colonial days of a Tingnall lady from France gives rise to the thought that possibly the name was given a French pronunciation. In that case the two main spelling variants would be of little importance to an English speaker. In French the first 'n," if present, would nasalize the first vowel, while the 'gn" could be understood as a single consonant sound like the English 'ny' and the resultant French sound would be close to 'Tanyall' in Eng. pronunciation. When spoken with *English* pronunciation, on the other hand, the first vowel ends with a hard 'g' (as in 'pig') and the 'n' before it, if present, would change the sound to 'ting-' (as in 'sing')--a considerable difference.

[183] And Daughters of the American Colonists, *Lineage Book II*. This source also gives Penelope's year of d. as 1811, and says that the ms. of Francis and Mary took place in 1755.

[184] *NC Estate Files, TJ jr & sr p. 31.* The sons **John C.** and TJ having d. (before the Feb 1813 session of the Wake Co. court), his living brothers and sisters and the chen of the dec'd TJ jr. petitioned the crt for a distribution of the land; the pet. failed as the assets were of less value than the sum due the ex. (S.a. *Wake crt recs II/108).*

[185] AAW in McSwain p. 209. AAW also says that the Fanning who m. (1) Mary Bustian and (2) Nancy Jeffreys had 2 sons, The *NC Estate Files* also list a Fanning who d. c1878 in Newhope Township in Chatham Co.; his wife was **Elizabeth**, and *Wake Co. M. Bonds* show a m. of Fanning Jones to **Betsey Penny** on 19 Nov 1829.

[186] *1860 fedcen* (another Fanning?)

Jones, Sally Jones (Mary) Jones, Penelope Jones (1805-78) m. **Alexander McKnight**, but Peggy Jones[187] [According to the newspaper 'Star'(from *M & D Notices from Raleigh Newspapers*, m. **Rich Smith,** her gr'fa is **Col. TJ].**

    5. **Mary ('Polly')** m. **Charles Stuart**; son: **Tingnall Stuart** (b. bef Aug 1807)
    6. **Penelope ('Penny')** m **Duncan Stuart**; son: Tingnall Stuart (b. bef Aug 1807)
    7. **Elizabeth ('Betsy')** m. (l) **Charles Briggs** cl788, (2) **Col. Absalom Alston** (cl8O3-1829).[188]
    8. **Deliah** m. **Westwood A. Jones**; chen incl dau (who m. __Scasboro) chen: twins **Tignal** & Penny [AAW: aka '**Jack**'] (who m. _Smith; ch m. _).
    9. **John C.** d. 11 Sep 1808 dsp. w. in Wake Co. pr. May 1810. Est. set'mnt 1812.

Notes: AAW adds that Fanning had 2 sons, **David and Fanning,** and that a 3rd Fanning was the bro of **John Ridley Jones**

The *NC Estate Files* (for Penny) confirm Martha as widow of Redding and mention the 3 daus **Martha, Mary B.,** and **Sally,** and 4 sons **TJ, John R., Fanning,** and **Thos,. Martha** m. **Francis Childs** (p. 33). **William Hill** was gdn of Mary and Sarah.

The *1860 fedcen for Wake, NC* shows a Fanning Jones b. 1826. It names **Redding, Sarah,** and **Mary.** This must be another Fanning, not the son or grson of TJ & his wife Penney.

Charles Stuart [or Stewart] and **Duncan Stuart** were brothers, and both had sons named Tingnall.

Contrary to CWD, AAW has the chen of **Tignal/King** as **Dr. John Jones** who m. **Mary K. Crisp, Hartwell, Tignal, Redding, Thomas,** and 2 daus.

The 1807 w. of their father Tingnal, Sr. (husband of Penny Cain), who was aged c70 or more at that time, states that he had given land to his sons Francis, Tingnall Jones Jr., Fanning, and Redding; we know also that the four daus were all m., that he had more than seven grandchen at that time, and that his son Tingnall, Jr., had predeceased him and rec'd from his fa 'the upper track (sic) on Crabtree Creek.' Evidently only young son **John C.** had not

---

[187] In the *No'ton, NC court, Dec Term 1817*, the chen of TJ Jr. pet'd for a division of the land left by their fa, who d. intestate. But s.a. the pet. (in JJ section) of 1813 by the chen of John Jones and the chen of this TJ.
[188] **Ab. Alston** is from Chowan Co. He m. Eliz in Wake Co. [Boddie, *Southern* ...VII/83]

received any land from his father before the latter's d.   John C. apparently d. rather young and had rec'd no land from his father except by bequest; the bequest, however, could never have been carried out since John predeceased his mother. Judging from all indications, the years of b. of the chen prob were c1750 - c1775. **John C.** may have had a physical affliction; he stated in his w. that he was 'of sound mind and memory,' but no comment refers to any possible physical problems.

The progeny of the chen of this family is shown as set forth in the chart by Camilla W. Davis.

Related or Unrelated

Misc. *Wulfeck* **Jones, Matthew** & wife **Martha Tignall** history **Francis** (son) m **Mary Ridley**   Wulfeck cites *11Tylers33* Schreiner- Yantis / pps 575 & 576   **Jones, Tignal (Cpt. Tinqual) [III?]** *VA census*   *1787*

Bockstruck / 23?   **Jones, Tignal, Sr.   Capt. militia   11 Mar 1765 Robt. Munford, Lt. Col.**

1790 f.c./33   Jones, Tignal Jr.   1st col, 20% dn. 6 whites, 24 blks.

1850 fedcen 'Tignel'   b. 1811 NC

*1870 fedce*n b. 1811, NC   residence Jackson, TX

Web: *Lawrence Co. AL, Bu. Index*   TJ b. 26 Jun 1811, d. 21 Apr 1887

US, Find A Grave   b.28 Jun 1811 Wake Co., d. 21Apr 1887, Colbert Co., AL

Bockstruck/137   Jones, Tignal Sgt   (Tingle) militia 1774 Dunmore's War

6T131   Jones, Tignal   Rev War   **Albridgton,** bro "officers"

TX, Muster ... **Tignal W Jones** 1861 military

US, IRS Tax ... TJ in TX 1866

1870 fedcen TJ b. 26 Jun 1811 in NC, other Jackson, TX

AL, Ws. and Pr.Recs c1882 in Colbert, AL

Boddie, Hist... VII82   **Jones, Tignal** d. 29 Aug 1807 "at his death oldest magistrate on Bench"   "b. 1735   Rev War, memb Comm .of Safety, Sheriff, etc"

6T46 **Jones, James Alfred** cites *"Eminent Reps of VA..."* dau: **Mary Morris Jones**; she m. **Judge D.G. Tyler**. s.a.
13WM143 bro: **Col. Robert Tingnall Jones**

Minutes, Hse of Commons /1079 TJ shff of Wake Co., NC 1786-7

9T283 Jones, Tignal **Robert Starkey** "yngst son of **William Armistead**, grson or gr'cousin, grson of **Ridley J**. He & TJ moved to TX c1850

TJ Jr. b. 1746, m. **Martha Anderson,** d. aft 26 Apr 1794

Dr. TJ Jr. m. **Mary A. Perk[l]inson** 9 Dec 1831 Prince Edward, VA [So'n Co.]? *[VA ms.1785-1940] FHL*

NY, Genealogical ... TJ in Hillsborough, NY 1775

Texas, Muster Roll Index Cards, 1838-1900 show a **Tignal W. Jones** for 1861. *US Find A Grave Index* shows the dates as 25 Nov 1820-18 Jun 1882, and the bu at Tyler, TX.

The fedcen for 1880 shows a Tignal Jones 68, in Saints, Colbert, AL; b. c1812. , wife Martha, 62. Fa [His w. of Aug 1882 is there in vol A] s.a. *Al, Wills and Probate Recs, 1753-1999*

1850 fedcen Franklin, AL. TJ, 39, b. c1811 in NC. Names are **Susan Jones, 37; TJ,14; JJ,13; Hartwell 10; Reading, 7; Martha 4; Mary, 4** mos.

1860 fedcen TX names **TJ (Lingual), 48; Susan 45; Reden 16;Pattie 13;Mary 10;Sue 8; Amy 3;Thos. Jones 3; John C. Jones 22; Holmes K. Jones 20.** (TJ b. c1812 in Wake, 1860 home Jackson, TX

1870 fedcen Jackson TX. chen: **Redding, 24; Martha, ?; Mary, 18; Lillie 15; Thos. ,12.**

TX, Death Certificates, 1903-1982. **Lillie Jones**, 82, b. 7 Jun 1855 in AL, d. 10 Dec 1937, her fa **('Signal') & mother Susan King** b. in [Raleigh], NC, Bu place for TJ, 75, [b. c1862] Lawrence, AL.

These last 3 recs seem to show that this family lived in AL & TX (the fa & mother b. in NC), that Susan (King?) d. between 1850 and 1870, and that **Thomas** was b. c1858. But the dates for TJ are not correct; there seems to be a confusion re the d.s of **TJ and Lillie**, but another rec. [*U.S.. Find A Grave Index* shows a TJ b. 26 Jul 1811, bu (d. ?) 21 Apr 1887 at Gonzales, TX; and another rec in the same source says Colbert Co., AL; these dates indicate d. at age 75]. A 3rd source, *Lawrence Co., AL, Burial Index* shows the bu in that Co. – in semi agreement wi the previous rec. *US Find A Grave Index* also shows in one report the mother of this TJ as **Martha**, the wife as Susan King?, the chen as **Lillie**; an infant; **Martha**; and **Thos Benjamin**, and in a 2nd report the names of chen as **Susan, Hartwell King**, and **John Curtis**.

US Find A Grave Index shows 6 burials for TJ in TX incl Tignal Jones & 3 in the period Dec-1875 to 31 Jan 1960 at Bastrop, TX.

Bentley, .../162   TJ m . **Emily High**

Chatham   *1790 fedcen*/88-9   Jones, Tignal [Sr?]
Chatham Co., NC   near **Elisha Cain, Arthur & Francis Jones**

ECC   *6T128*   Jones, Vinkler & Eliz. interest in estate of **Westwood [Armistead]**; her bros: **Tingnall, Harwood** (in 1790 he & Ting. lived in Granville Co. - in Northam., NC). Judgemnt for 7 Oct 1766

6T130   **Jones, Lydia**   w. pr   28 Oct 1773   Eliz.City Co.
bros: **John, Tingnall, Harwood, Vinkler, Francis** ; siss: **Marg, Jane Armistead** of Lancaster/Thompson   ncs etc {**Jane Armistead** m. 8 Dec 1770 in Lancaster Co, VA [*VA, Select Ms. 1785-1940*]), and resided in Charles Parish [*York Co., VA, Charles Parish Recs, 1648-1789*]

Edgecombe   *NC archives*   Jones, Francis   w. rec 1755
Edgecombe Co., NC   wife: **Mary**;   chen: **Nath'l, Tingnall, Matthew, Francis, Albr., John, Bette Day, Lydia, Ridley[?], Jemima, Lucy, Mary** et al

Granville   *6T128*   Jones, Vinkler & Eliz.   judgmnt for 7 Oct 1766
Eliz City Co.   interest in estate of **Westwood [Armistead]**; **Tingnall, Harwood** he & Ting. lived in Granville Co. (in 1790 in Northamton, NC)

Hampton   *6T128+130*   **Jones Lydia**   w. pr. 28 Oct 1773
Hampton   sons: **TJ, Harwood, Francis, John, Vinkler**;   Sisters: **Marg.Thompson, Eliz.Armistead**; ncs, cns

IoW *9T137* m. **Martha Anderson**; mother: **Mary**; Grprnts: **Matthew & Martha Harwood**. Wife, **Mary**; Bro., MJ d. 1762. Cites *6T45*.

Meckl' *Elliot, .../75* TJ Sr m. bond 16 Nov 1767 to **Sarah**, dau of Thos. Anderson

Bockstruck/23 **Jones, Tignal Sr. Cpt.** militia 8 Apr 1765
Mecklenburg Co. 11 Mar ?

VA Colonial Soldiers TJ Sr. Cpt. of militia 8 Apr 1765

*Bockstruck*23 Jones, Tignal (Cpt....Sr.) oath 8 Apr 1765

All of the following 10 entries apparently refer to the same person:

1790 f.c./ 33 **Jones Tignal Jr.** census 1790 Mecklenburg Co. 6 white males & 16... +24 blacks

Wills III/227 TJ Jr. w. 21 Jun 1793 wits incl **Martha Anderson, wife;** sons: **Thos., Harwood, James, Tignall;** daus unnamed; friend TJ'. Codicil 26 Apr '94, rec Oct '94

TJ moved to Meck Co. sometime bef the Rev and his w. is at Boydton dated 21 Jun 1793, pr 13 Oct 1794. `

6T45 Jones, Tingnall to Mecklenburg Co., VA prior to Rev War m. Martha Anderson, dau of **Thos. Anderson** He called himself, Tingnall Jones, Junior.

VA. an uncompleted codicil, attested to by **Sarah Anderson** et al. w. ex by "friend" Tignal

Elliott, Early... 9 **Anderson, Thos Junr.** W 9 Dec 1793 Mecklenburg Co., VA. dated 8 Apr 1793 Sarah (wife?); Tignal Jones, Jr., exor et al. Martha Jones, mother cites *WBk 3/187*: W of **Thos Anderson, Jr.**

1790 f.c./32 **Jones, Tignal (Tegnal) Sr.** lists several **Tignors**, a **Hardy Jones** Last col., 80% down. On p 155 of index. [A Hardy Jones is also listed in Nansemond Co. 14 Oct 1752 A TJ calls himself Jr, names wife Martha, sons **Thos, Anderson, HJ, Matt, Wm, TJ.**

WB 3/240 TJ est appr by TJ Oct 1794; exs Martha Jones, Thomas A. Jones...

9T137   **Jones, Tingnall** [w. 1794]   m. **Martha Anderson** [w. 1831]; mother **Mary;** grprnts Matthew & Martha Harwood   cites *6T45&46*.   Bro: **Matthew**

Elliott, Early... 167   Jones, Tignal, Jr   est appr Oct 1794 Mecklenburg Co., VA.   exs: **Martha Jones, Thos. A. Jones** et al   cites *W Bk 3/240*.   Appr. by Tignal [III?], et al

Elliott, Early...51   Jones, Tignal, Junr,   d. 26 Apr 1794 Mecklenburg Co., for processioning of land.]

6T46   Jones, Tingnall   sheriff Warw. Co. 1761   to NC ca.1776 then Mecklenb. Co., VA   d. 5 Apr1802.   **Francis, Jno; Martha Hopkins, Sarah A. Boyd**   rep Wake Co. in Prov. Congress; w. rec 13 Jun 1802

Wills V/52-4   TJ gr'dau: **Sarah Jones Hopkins**   w. 5 Apr 1802, rec Jun 1803. Dau **Sarah A.** m. **Robt Boyd.**   Son **Richd B, Francis, John** (<21); dau: **Martha C. Hopkins** (husb. In KY)

TJ *(XIIIWM143)* rep Wake Co. in the Provincial Congress of 1776, then moved to Meck. Co.; his w. dated 13 Jun 1802 names Francis,   C. Martha C. Hopkins, JJ, grchen Sarah Jones and Rich Boyd [189]

1850 FEDCEN   TJ age 60, plus **William H Jones 30, Augusta Jones 18, Tignal J Morton 7, Martha Morton 5, Harriet Morton 4.** Meckl. Co.

1850 fedcen   Jones, Tignal (Tingnall)   Mecklenburg Co. 22nd reg.

Schreiner-Yantis   Cpt. 1787

VA, Compiled Census and Census Substitutes Index, 1607-1890 Meck. Co. No town listed. 1779.

Wulfeck *Ms ... I /4 /58*   **MJ**   m. **Mary Lee**; his prnts **Matthew Jones & Martha Harwood**   res. York Co.; ,   cites *11 T 33*

VA, Co. M. Recs   m. bond of 16 Nov 1767 by **TJ & TJ Jr. m. to Sarah Anderson**

VA, COUNTY M. Recs   Consent of 18 Apr by **TJ** for m. of his dau Sarah Anderson [Jr] to **Robt. Boyd**

---

[189] From *6T147*

W. 5 Apr 1802   Meckl.   Dau Sarah A. m. Robt Boyd, sons **Richd B, Francis, John** (<21); **Martha C. Hopkins** (husb in KY); a dau rec Jun 1803. Mentions no wife, **Thos.J**, cuz **WmTaylor**

W III Meckl 187   **Anderson, Thomas**   w. 8 Apr 1793   Meckl. Co., bro: **James** ; b-in-l **Tingnal Jr;** mother: **Sarah**   wit: "**Martha Jones, Junior.**"

Elliott, Early... 9   **Anderson, Thos. [Sr.]**   w. 8 May 1780   Meckl. Co., VA.   Wife: **Sarah**; daus: **Sarah [Anderson] Jones, Martha Jones.**   2 daus m. 2 Joneses

WB 3/187   W. of Jr.. 9 Dec 1793. Mother Sarah; bro-in-law TJ Jr.

W XII Meckl 446   Jones, Martha.   one son-in-l: **William J Pattillo** w. 2 Sep 1831   Meckl. Co., VA. dau Frances A Feild   sons: **Harwood, James, Tingnal**; daus: **Mary A Feild, Martha Pattillo**   codicil 3 Oct 1831, rec 17 Oct; Martha's son **James Anderson**

Wills 18 Meck /214   **Jones Tingnal Dr.**   legatee 4 Aug 1823 Meckl. Co., VA   w. of **Mariana Blackburn**

Wills 18 Meck 509+   Jones, Tingnall.   dau **Harriet/---Morton** !W 13 Nov 1852 "Roseland" Meckl. Co., VA. No wife nmed   chen: **William H., Harriet, Martha** m. **Victor M. Eppes**; nephew: **Jas. Alfred Jones.**   Harriet dec'd; her chen **Tingnal, Martha M, Harriet A.**

Wills 19 Meck 62-7   Jones, Tingnal Dr.   Acct   29 Sep 1856 Roseland Meckl. Co., VA   purchasers incl: **Dr. William H Jones, Winckler, Eppes,**   Acct for Roanoke plantation made 2 Oct 1856

Elliott, M. Recs. 1765-1810 of Meck. Co   75 **Jones, Tingnal [sic] Sr** M. Bond   16 Nov 1767   Meckl Co., VA   Sarah dau of **Thos Anderson** (wife)   surety: **Tingnal Jones, Jr.**

Elliott, M. Recs. 1765-1810 of Meck. Co. /66   **Jones, Martha Cary** m.   27 Jul 1796 **Edmund Hopkins**   consent: **Tignal** [sic] Jones, fa of **Martha**

Elliott, M. Recs. 1765-1810 of Meck. Co. 81   **Jones, Elizabeth** M. Bond.   25 Feb 1794   Meckl. Co., VA   **Robert Lewis** husb consent: **Tignal Jones, fa of Eliz.**

9T282   **Jones, Tingnall** (son of 'cozen Matt.')   sheriff 1761   Warwick Co., VA. his neph: **Tingnall, Jr.** "The 'Sr' of the Mecklenburg w. of 5 Apr 1802. " Grandneph: **Jno. Armistead, Jr** .

VA Col. Soldiers 23   **Jones, Tignal Sr.** Cpt militia 8 Apr 1765 Mecklenburg Co., VA

Elliott, Early... 32 Jones, Tignal, Sr. wit   Mecklenburg Co., VA. wi **Jas. Anderson**   cites *W Bk I/396*

1820 fedcen   Dr 'Tiznal' Jones   7 Aug 1820

Sussex   *D B F P 437 Sussex Co Recs*   Jones, Tignal service 1775

Wake M . & D. Notices from NC Newspapers /110   **Jones, Penelope** (gr.dau of Jones, Col. Tignal)   m . (date and place not given this page)   entry says "see **Smith, Richard**".

UA, Fed. Cen. Mortality ...   TJ b. 1789. In Mar 1850 in Wake

NC, index to M. Bonds   23 Jan 1825 [to Emily High]

TJ 25 Sep 1849 wife Emiline M.; R.   Vinkler R., John   P., sons

Broughton, NC M. & D.....I ? 117   Jones, Col. Tignal [III?]   m. 25 Jan 1825   Wake Co. **Emily High**

Broughton, NC M. & D.....133   Jones, Jr., Tignal d. May 1807 Wake Co.   son's d. RB-7/295 AR.

1830 fedcen, Wake

1840 fedcen, Wake

1860 fedcen TX   names **TJ (Lingual), 48, Susan 45, Reden 16, Pattie 13, Mary 10, Sue 8, Amy 3, Thos. Jones 3;   John C. Jones 22, Holmes K. Jones 20.** (TJ b. c1812 in Wake, 1860 home Jackson, TX

Clark, Col. Soldiers...830 Jones, Tignal   Lt. 6 Oct 1773   Wake Co. militia

NC Col. & State Recs.   JonesTignal   JP   1776   Wake XXIII/995   links 3 Jones

NC Col. & State Recs.   **Jones, Tignal**   militia Lt. Col. XXVIII (Index?)

Wheeler, History...I 78   Jones, Tignal   rep 4 Apr 1776   Halifax [for Wake Co.] s.a. Cain, *Provincial Congress;* **Elisha Cain** rep Chat'm Co.

Wheeler, History I/416 Jones, Tignal   delegate   21 Aug 1775 Hillsboro [rep of Wake Co.]   *Provincial Congress of NC.*   s.a. pps 499,500

*Wheeler, History...*I 421 JonesTignal   Hse Commons 1777   NC [rep Wake Co.], *General Assembly*   s.a. entry 186.

*Wheeler, History...*I 421   Jones, Tignal (Tignall) rep   1797 NC *General Assembly* (rep Wake Co)   followed by **Nathan'l, Kimbro', Seth, Wesley Jones**

Mitchell, NC   Jones,Tignal   w.1850 Wake Co., NC   s.a. *I/326*

*Haun, ...Land...*43/160-1/#475   Jones, Tignal   3 Aug 1778   N side Beaver Cr., Wake Co., NC   200 acs of **Thos. Mann** join his line

[There are at least 20 land entries in this source, mostly acquisitions by TJ beginning in 1778, but extending later to incl lands of **John, Jas., Nathaniel, Seth and TJ Jr.**]

6T46   Jones, Tingnall   sheriff Warw 1761   to NC c1776 then Mecklenb. Co., VA   W d. 5 Apr 1802.   **Francis , Jno; Martha Hopkins ,Sarah A.Boyd**   rep Wake Co. in Prov. Congress; w. rec 13 Jun 1802

9T 282   Jones, **Nathaniel & Tignal** (sons of **Francis & M**)   fedcen 1790   Wake Co., NC   Newman doesn't believe Tig. is the Tignall in Meck "among largest slaveholder in the county." 1782+. [Both served in the Wake Co. militia; **TJ as Lt, NJ** as Capt.]

Wake Co. Bk7 /295+   Jones, Tingnall. Some chen dead?   W. rec Nov 1807   Wake Co., NC.   wife: **Penny**; sons: Francis, Tingnall Jr., **Reading, Fanning, John**; daus: **Eliz.**; grdau: **Penny** (dau of Westwood), 2 grsons: [both named **Tingnall Stuart**]

Wheeler, History of NC [vol. I /86] shows MJ apptd major Apr 1776   in Chatham Co., NC   [34 mi W of Raleigh]. Chatham Co. & Guilford Co. formed from Orange 1770.

The *1790 fedcen* pp 87, 49 for <u>Hillsborough Dist</u> shows **MJ** in a household of 3 wh. males and 3 wh. fem. The same fedcen shows a **TJ** pp 88 & 104.

1790 fedcen pps 88,114; Hillsborough Dist,, Wake – 2 2 3, 39 slaves

Wtlls, Wake TJ w. dated 1849 wife: **Emiline**, sons: **Vinkler R,, John P.**

23 Jan 1825 TJ m. Emily High in Wake Co. [*Wake Co. Crt recs.*]. Bondsman: **Francis A. Jones** [and *NC, Index to M. Bonds, 1741-1868*]

b. 1789 NC, d. Mar 1850, age 61. Wake [*US fedcen Mortality Schedules Index, 1850-1880*] c1821 NC, Wake [*NC, Ws & Pr. Recs,1665-1998*]

NC Estate Files: TJ's wife __ **Semmes**; 1817 Nor'ton Co. pet. of chen
ı
Son of Penelope Cain; wife **Peggy**; chen Penelope Cain, Moore [sp?] [*1800 fedcen*] 'Fignal'

NC Digital Collection, Family Records: **Robert Tignal Jones** m. **Lucy Maria Jones** 8 Feb 1843. She rem. in1870

6T46 cites *"Eminent Reps of VA...* and *s.a. 13WM143.* says **James Alfred Jones** was bro of **Col. Robert Tingnall Jones.** **Mary Morris** m. **Judge D.G. Tyler.**

US, Find A Grave b.28 Jun 1811 Wake Co., d. 21Apr 1887, Colbert Co., AL. Another entry in this source: b. in Raleigh, other (d.) in Gonzales Co., TX

Minutes Gov's Council in New Bern v. 12/600 TJ jp and Comm of Peace in Orange Co. 4 Nov 1769

Warwick XIII/143 TJ apptd Sheriff 6 Aug 1761 Warwick

WM XIII 144 Jones, Tignal 1761 orphan of Matthew Jones, ward of HJ

John Tingnall-- below Waters Creek. pp 340, 342 *of Order Book.*

An orp. of JJ, **Eliz.** 'to be put to school at cost of her est.' (/371) 1 Mar1753]

York *6T146* **Jones, Harwood** mention 20 Jul 1778 York Co., VA York Co. Recs. ref to **Wm. Harwood, Tingnall Jones,** exors

York#4 Order Bk. 1774-84/167 Jones, Tignal, exor for Jones, Harwood record 20 Jul 1778 to 15 Feb 1779 (p.203) motion of TJ & Wm. Harwood

Jane Armistead m. 8 Dec 1770 in Lancaster Co, VA [*VA, Select Ms. 1785-1940*], and resided in Charles Parish [*York Co., VA, Charles Parish Recs, 1648-1789*]

Redding

NC Estate Files: d. testate 27 Dec 1815. Wake. Widow: **Martha.** Chen: **John R., Mary B., Martha, Sarah, Thos., TJ, Fanning M. Martha Jr.** m. **Francis Child**

1800 fedcen/130   **Jones, Redding**   Wake Co. (743)

1810 fedcen/135   Jones, Redding   Ons 77?

Haun, Wake Co. Land .../147/466/#38   **Jones, Nathaniel (WP)**   land 5 Mar 1816 E fork of Black Cr., Wake Co., NC   & **Redding. Nathl (CT)** wit.   **Henry Jones (CT)** enters 400 acs adj HEIRS of Nathl

Haun, Wake Co. Land .../153, 481/#113   Jones, Tignal, Jr, dec'd. Apr 1882   Marks Branch, Wake Co., NC   100 acs adj heirs of Tingnal and of Redding Jones

NC Est Files – Wake -- lists 'Reddin Jones (1879)' for a Reddin who d. intestate;   sister: **Miss Mary F.** aged c45

Fedcen 1860] Wake; b. 1826; mentions Redding, Sarah, Mary.

Wake Co. M . Bonds /269: A Redding Jones m. **Catherine Roles** 23 Jan 1840

Fanning

[*Find a Grave*] (26 Nov 1812 - 13 Feb 1865 MS).

[*Fedcen 1860*] Wake; b. 1826; mentions Redding, Sarah, Mary.

William

The first William Jones we encounter in this line in Warwick Co. is 6 Apr 1749 (/289) when he served on a grand jury, which would mean a b. date of 1728 or before. There are 4 other mentions in the existing Warwick Co. Court records until the entry of 4 Jan 1753 (/364) citing the d. of William Jones which was probably in 1752. A rec. of c1728 from the NC colonial courts [*State Archives of NC*] shows JJ and **Henry Jones** as exs. of their fa William Jones. No records tell us who his parents were, but we can rule out the William whose w. was 1766 (son of **Matthew [IV] of York Co.**) and all those who lived apparently exclusively in NC.

A William Jones b. 22 Dec 1770 [*VA Bs. & Christenings, 1584-1917*] was the son of **JJ & Anna B.** in Surry, VA.

William Jones, son of the **Albridgton Jones** of the 1784 w. in Southampton Co., was ward of Nathaniel Jones Sr. after his fa d. The record also names his sister **Jemimah**. In the codicil of 1785 he makes his son Albridgton gdn to William – indicating that William was under age in 1785 and Albridgton had just become 21, as he wasn't in the 1784 body of the will, setting his b. at 1734. [See the section on Matthew II.]

A William Jones is named [*Rootsweb*] as the son of **Vinkler** and **Eliz. Armistead** and husband of **Eliz. Norman** whom he m. c1808 at Oxford, NC. Chen: T.**P. Eppes Armistead Jones** m. 1835 **Mary Frances Hawkins** (their chen: **William, Westwood Jones, James Jones** who m. **Eliz. Johnson, Mary Jones** m. (1) __Foster, (2) John Burnell; **Lucy Jones.** m. **Richard Harris, Betty Jones, John Jones, Armistead Jones** of Raleigh, NC, and **Thos Norman Jones**

1810 fedcen for War. Co. William Jones 3 males under 10, 1 male 26-45, 1 45 up; 1 fem. under 10

Edwin C. Dunn, paper on Wm. Bressie [c1626-1701], William Jones recd gift from **Susannah Bressie** (his aunt?) 12 Mar 1701

In the 19th century we encounter yet another William Jones and his son, William Jones, in Warwick Co. (See above the will in the succession of wills). 'Sr.' made his will 13 Jun 1824 and the pr. was 9 Dec 1824.

The **Carter Burwell** (16 Oct 1773 JCC – 9 Feb 1819 JCC) in the w. had siblings **Lucy Randolph** (1777-1810), **Philip** (1776-1849), **Nathaniel** (1779-1849), **Lewis**

Edwin C. Dunn, paper on Wm. Bressie [c1626-1701], William Jones recd gift from **Susannah Bressie** (his aunt?) 12 Mar 1701

In the 19th century we encounter yet another William Jones and his son, William Jones, in Warwick Co. (See above the will in the succession of wills). 'Sr.' made his will 13 Jun 1824 and the pr. was 9 Dec 1824.

The **Carter Burwell** (16 Oct 1773 JCC – 9 Feb 1819 JCC) in the w. had siblings **Lucy Randolph** (1777-1810), **Philip** (1776-1849), **Nathaniel** (1779-1849), **Lewis** (1781-1782), **Dr. Lewis** (1783-1826), **Robert Carter** (1785-1813), and **Wm.** (1782-

1782). Carter was also half brother of: **William Nelson (1791-1822), Tayloe Page (1789-1811), Susanna Grymes Burwell (1792-1793), Mann Page (1793-1794), Eliz. Gwynn Hay (1795-1855), Mary Whiting (1798-1880), George Harison Burwell (1799-1873), William Nelson (1789-1822),** and **Thos Hugh Nelson Burwell (1805-1841).**   [All surnames are Burwell except that the husbands' names are shown for the m. females.]   [Source: *Find A Grave.com*]

In 1873, **William Benjamin Jones** (1825-11 Feb 1878), clerk of the Warwick County Circuit Court for a decade prior to the Civil War then again 1866-1878, had given land for a church in Warwick County [*deed copy at Ft. Eustis communicated by **Dr. Chris McDaid***]. See also the info provided by McSwain in her pps. 227-232.

The 1890 fedcen for Wake Co. shows the family of **William R. Jones and wife Mary C.** with chen incl a **Wm** and **Lidia** of 4 yrs.

The Jones-Pointer Bible (NC Digital Collections) shows a m. of William Jones to **Grizzell** 1776.   [p.88] Dower: lands of **William Jones & Albridgton Jones** where **John Jones** lived. NJ d. intestate c1816

York Deeds, Orders, Wills, etc #13, 1706-? William Jones church absence   24 Jun 1707

A William Jones was constable for upper p'cincts of Bruton Par. until 24 May 1705 -*York Dds, Ords, Ws #21/327.*

York, Dds & Bnds 1713-1729 /173?   William Jones of Bruton Par.   grantee 14 Feb 1714

York Ord. Bk 12/20, 1829-35   William Jones dec'd of War.   c1830

York, Ords & Ws 1716-1720/73   William Jones of Bruton Par grantee 40 acs plantation in Indian field, N side of Queen's Creek, no wife mentioned 14 Feb 1714.

Appendix I   Wake Co. Court Recs

These court minutes provide much other information about 'our' Joneses:

Bk I (1777-1784) /19: '**Alb. Jones** ... esq. ,[190] Justice....'
A-1/1: 4 Jun 1771 [1777?]: **Tingnal** to take list of taxables in **Capt. Nathaniel Jones**' district.
A-1/4: **Tignal Jones** cattlemark a swallofork in the right ear and a slit in the left.
A-1/5: spelled again **'Tingnall'**
A-1/6: **Matthew Jones'** place mentioned; also Swift Creek.
II/l: **Tignal Jones [Jr.]**, Sheriff. [
II/42: Mentions **Col. Tingnall Jones**
II/108: **Redding Jones** [son of **Tingnall,Sr.**], juror with **Charles Briggs**.
II/37: ordered that **Nathll Jones, Sr.**, be guardian to **Wm. & Jemimah Jones**, orphans of **Albrighton Jones** dec'd
II/62: **David Bell** exhibited his account for disbursements, etc against **Jemimah, Wm., Penny Hardy** and **Willis Jones**,[191] orphans of **Albridgton Jones**, dec'd.
II/13: **Tingnal Jones.**, Esq ... Sheriff of Wake Co. (4 Sep 1787). Tingnall and **John Jones**, security.
II/25 **Tingnall** Sr. and Jr. together [s.a. *III/43, III/1041*]
II/99: Deed from 'Western' **[Westwood] A. Jones** to Paton Sledge Oath of **Willie Jones**.[192] (Sep 1792)
III/13: **Tignal Jones, Jr.** and **Charles Briggs**, Esquires, on a committee.
III/36: Commissioners of Peace and Justices
III/54: **Tignal, Sr.** and **Charles Briggs** on a committee of three.
III/54: Administration on estate of John Jones, dec'd, is granted to **Willie Jones** who came into court... with **Tignal Jones, Sr.**, and **Nathaniel Jones** C.T. [Crabtree] [This John Jones who d. bef Dec 1794, was not John C. Jones, son of **Tingnall**, as John C. wrote his w. 11 Sep 1808, the year after his father d.]
III/54: Ordered that **Tignal Jones**, Sr., be allowed the sum of £ 2 14 3 per year as long as he keeps the bridge on Crab Tree at his house in passable order.

---

[190] It may be noted that 'esquire' was emblematic of very high distinction in the early Colonial Period and into the post-Revolution, prob reserved for governors, convention delegates and others of high elected office. 'Gentleman' indicated a person of 'quality,' who did not do manual labor.

[191] This Willis might be the one who d. in 1852, a res. of MS. [NN Recs], or he might have d. c. 1819 in NC

[192] *6T131*: Willie d. at home of NJ in Raleigh. [*NADAR*/499: Willie Jones fr Halifax Co. in Prov. Congress 21 Aug 1775; delegate wi **Elisha Cain**.] A Willie Jones m. **Penelope** 28 Dec 1809 [*NC Collection, U of NC, Chapel Hill*] and there were 2 men of that name in Wake Co. in the *1800 fedcen*.

III/61: **Charles Briggs Tingnal Jones, Nathaniel Jones Sr. & Jr.**: a committee appointed to divide the estate of **John Jones** [for inheritance purposes]. Dec. 1794.
III/64: **James Jones** appointed guardian to **Polly Ridly Jones**, orphan of **John Jones** dec'd.[193]
III/89: **Albridgton Jones** ordered to jury duty c1795.
III/95: **Redding Jones** on jury c1795.
IV/33: mention of 'Fannen' **[Fanning] Jones.**
IV/166: **Wm Jones** orphan of **James Servant Jones.**
V/41: **Matthew Jones** came into court.
V/41: inventory of estate of **John Jones**. Appointment of widow, **Mary Jones** as administratrix.

> *Notes* The brothers **AJ, TJ, MJ, NJ, and JJ** had moved to Wake Co. either with their spouses (as was the case with at least TJ and JJ) or they m. in NC and raised their families there. All of them or their chen became involved in some way with local gov't; NJ Jr. was sheriff for Wake Co. by c1784 or bef.

NC, Will and Probate Records, 1665-1998: This source shows that **Albridgton** ('Albritain' here) d. c1789, that Nathl Sr. was ex. of his (NJ Sr's) fa's estate as well as gdn to Albridgton's chen **William & Jemima** [she was in school 4 Mar 1791, so b. 1785 or before]. William was a ward 17 Sep 1797 [thus b. 1777 or bef.]. **David Bell** became gdn in 1792. **Matthew Jones** was mentioned in the estate papers as well as the crt recs shown above; he lived nearby [in Morrisville, N of Raleigh, where he and his wife are bu.] NJ Sr (CT) and Jr are both mentioned. The mention of 10 months board for **Willis Jones** noted in 1795, suggests that he became of age 1795 or 1796, thus b. c1769 or 1770]. There was a m. Willis Jones to **Ruth Banks** 8 Sep 1789 this could be the same person.

These orph accounts were all filed and examined in Wake Co. and recorded in the Clerk's office in *Bk C /367-8* on 11 Jan 1794. McSwain (her /196) gives *Bk 2 /15-17* as a record of Albridgton's w. of 25 Nov 1787, but I did not see that source. Also a *Pedigree Resource File* in Ancestry.com gives the b. of this Albridgton as c11 Jan 1745 in Isle of Wight Co., and the d. as c26 Nov 1787 in Wake Co., but I have not discovered a source for that info either. The *NC Estate Files* also show **Penny H[ardy] Jones** as orphan of Albridgton Jones on 19 Jan 1799 with **Nathaniel Jones [Jr.]** as guardian

---

[193] Refer to pet. of Feb 1813

Book E/345]. This source indicates that **Penny** was not 21 in 1799 and therefore was b. c1779 or later.

Appendix 2: *Charts from letters of Amelia Ann Whitaker*

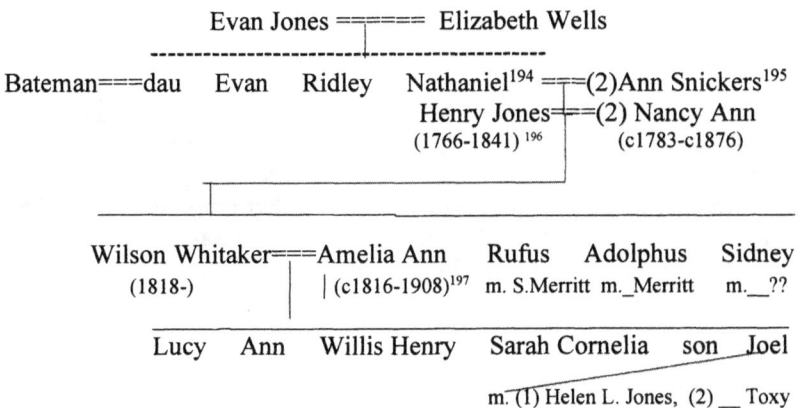

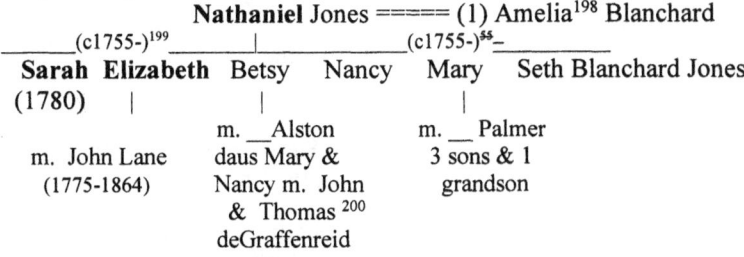

The first m. of Nathaniel:

```
                Nathaniel Jones ===== (1) Amelia198 Blanchard
      (c1755-)199       |            (c1755-)ss
Sarah Elizabeth   Betsy     Nancy      Mary    Seth Blanchard Jones
(1780)              |                    |
                 m.__Alston           m.__Palmer
m. John Lane     daus Mary &          3 sons & 1
(1775-1864)      Nancy m. John        grandson
                 & Thomas 200
                 deGraffenreid
```

---

[194] AAW: "**Grfa [Nathaniel - WP]** moved from Chowan River to White Plains...The WP place remained in the family until 1895," but then she says in two places that her fa was son of 'Nathaniel of Crabtree.'

[195] **Mrs. Whitaker's** letters include a seeming contradiction in apparently combining WP and CT family groups together. This graphic thus shows elements of both and is indeterminate with regard to the proper placement of Evan Jones.

[196] From CWD chart

[197] NC Recs

[198] '**Millicent**' in some sources.

[199] *Pedigree Resource File, FamilySearch.org*

[200] No recs were found for these names, but the 1794 will of Jr. in Lunenberg VA is listed [*VA wills and administrations 1632-1800*].

99

The two marriages of Henry Jones:

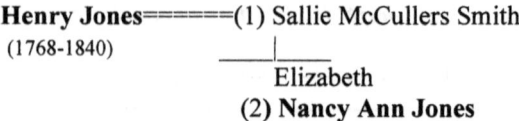

Henry Jones======(1) Sallie McCullers Smith
(1768-1840) |
          Elizabeth
(2) **Nancy Ann Jones**

Susie Gentry was the dau of **Mr. Gentry** (1832-) who m. **Martha Anne Jones** (1832-), and she was the grdau of **Dr. John Ridley Jones** (b. c1810) and **Martha Lane** (1815-); John R. was son of **Reading Jones** (1769-1815) and **Martha Bustian** (1785-1846); his maternal gr prnts were **John Lane** (1775-1864) and **Sarah Elizabeth Jones** (1780-). **Sarah** was dau of **Nat Jones** (1760-) and **Miss Blanchard** (1760-).

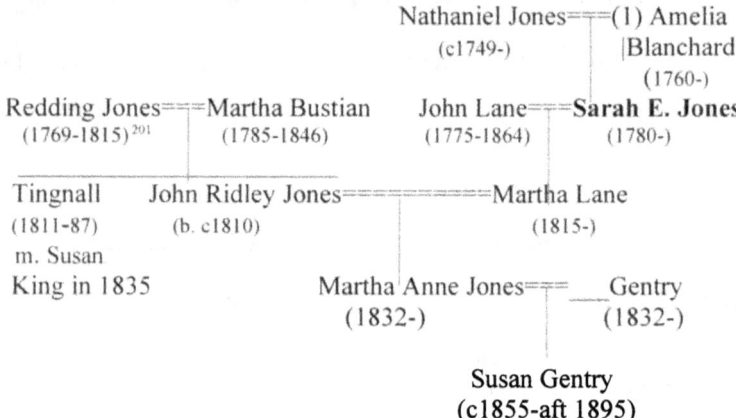

Nathaniel Jones===(1) Amelia
(c1749-) |Blanchard
                (1760-)

Redding Jones===Martha Bustian   John Lane===Sarah E. Jones
(1769-1815)[201] (1785-1846)   (1775-1864) (1780-)

Tingnall   John Ridley Jones===========Martha Lane
(1811-87)   (b. c1810)   (1815-)
m. Susan
King in 1835   Martha Anne Jones===   Gentry
                    (1832-)   (1832-)

            Susan Gentry
            (c1855-aft 1895)

[The following chart from AAW begins with a **Patsy Jones** who is prob **Martha**, dau of **Redding Jones and Martha Bustian** and a sister of **John Ridley Jones**

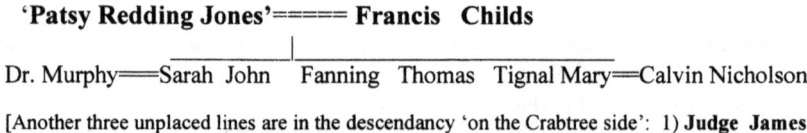

'**Patsy Redding Jones**'===== **Francis Childs**
                    |
Dr. Murphy===Sarah John Fanning Thomas Tignal Mary===Calvin Nicholson

[Another three unplaced lines are in the descendancy 'on the Crabtree side': 1) **Judge James Jones** of Texas; 2) '**James K. Jones of Ark**; and 3) '**George W. Jeffreys, Aunt Helen Jones**' first husband [who] m. a **Miss Hinton** first—in 1835.']

---

[201] The w. of this Redding was dated 26 Dec 1815; he d. the same day. The widow, **Martha**, and chen incl **Martha the younger, Fanning M., John R., & TJ** in pet. **Martha** m. **Francis Childs. FJ & John R.** were protectors of Redding's orphans **Mary B. and Sarah.**   *Estate Files ...Wake Co.*]

Appendix 3: CWD Jones chart of 1932

Despite the obvious mistakes or omissions at the beginning of this chart, it needs to be published. It is probably mostly correct, and it extends Jones genealogical data. Clearly much time and effort went into this work. The original, I believe, is in the Ft. Eustis library, and there are to me no known copies except my own. She cites as references court records of VA and NC, family histories, and tombstones w/o showing references to specific data, but a few references have been added here in brackets.

The form used here is not the drawing form (the usual 'tree' form of genealogies) of the original chart (which is much too large) but a prose version. For better readability, names of children are shown here in bold only where the child later marries *and* has children; generations are indicated here with the labels 1-4 (to show a starting point), then a,b,c, etc., in progressively reduced font sizes, and through indentations for successive generations also.

The beginning: Ms. Davis starts her chart with Matthew Jones I marrying Elizabeth. Albridgton Ridley, which is obviously a confusion of two generations, is thus totally incorrect, and therefore is omitted here. The balance of her chart is presented without any 'corrections.' In fact, this editor has endeavored to present this work as accurately as possible, verbatim in every detail after the initial confusion, without any 'improvements' or any changes of any kind except additions enclosed in square brackets.

***

1] Tingnall Jones Sr (will 1802) (son of Mary Tingnall) m. Sarah —in 1767; chen: [Fran]ces Jones, **John Wesley** Jones (Warren Co. NC) m. Ann Strechen, Martha C. Jones m. – Hopkins, **Sarah** Jones m. Robt Boyd, **Tingnall** m. ... , Betsy Jones, Mary Jones, & Henry Jones.
   a) John Wesley Jones and Ann Strechen had chen: **Alexander** Strechen Jones who m. Lucinda – in 1834, [an unnamed dau] who m. Victor Eppes, & **Ann** Jones who m. John J – Speed. [209]
      b) Alexander Strechen Jones & Lucinda – had ... Jones, [Al]ice Jones, John Tingnall Jones, Alex Jones, Sallie Jones, Robert Jones George F Jones, Earnest Jones, **Susan Blackwood** Jones (1846-1876) m. Waller E Taylor (b 1807) in 1871.

---

[209] [*Prestwould Chapter DAR, Marriage Recs 1811-1853 Meckl Co.* m. bond 19 Sep 1825]. {Fns 202-208 not in use}

  c)The chen of Susan Blackwood Jones & Waller E. Taylor were **Susie Blackwood** Taylor, & **Edward Wesley** Taylor (1872) m. Anna Mc--.
  b)The chen of Ann Jones & John J Speed were **Rosa Ann** Speed who m. Thomas Jefferson Taylor, and **Isabella** Speed who m. Dr. Hal Davis.
   c)The child of Rosa Ann Speed & Thomas J. Taylor was Waller Edmond Taylor (b 1847).
   c)The chen of Isabella Speed & Dr. Hal were Major John Davis, Alice Davis who m. Harry L. Wills, and William Davis
 a)The child of Sarah Jones & Robt Boyd was Richard Boyd.
 a)The child of Tingnall & -- was Elizabeth Jones who m. Robt. Lewis in 1794.

2] Matthew Jones IV (York Co.) (son of Mary Tingnall) m. Mary Lee. Chen: William Jones (w 1766), Lydia Jones (w 1773),[210] **Francis** Jones (w 1784) who m. Jane Armistead in 1770, **Harwood** who m. Elizabeth --, **Tingnall** Jones [Jr.] (W 1794) [In Mecklenburg Co. VA – *Torrence*] who m. Martha Anderson (w 1831), **Vinkler Jones** (b. c1771-w. 1817) who m. Elizabeth Armistead, John Jones, **Margaret** Jones who m. John Thompson, and Elizabeth Jones who m. John Armistead (w 1787).
 a) Francis Jones & Jane Armistead had [dau] who m. Robt Withe Nealson.
 a)Harwood Jones & Elizabeth -- had **John** Jones, **Harwood** Jones Elizabeth Jones, and **Ann** Jones.
 a)Tingnall & Martha Anderson had **Thomas A. Jones**
who m. Mary Crenshaw in 1799, Harwood Jones who m. Rachel Crenshaw in 1806,[211] **James B** Jones (d 1834) who m. Judith Bailey Hall, Matthew Jones, William (w 1814), **Dr. Tingnall** Jones (1790-1868)[212] who m. [1] Mary A—(d 1832) in 1831 and [2] Martha REG (1798-1828), **Martha** Jones who m. William — Patillo,[213] **Mary** Jones who m. – Feild,[214] and **Frances** Jones who m. – Feild.
  b) Thomas A Jones & Mary Crenshaw had James H Jones, Ann Jones, Thomas Jones, Osmond Jones, Eveline Jones, Lucy Jones, Frances Jones, Sarah Jones, Melville Jones, Thaddeus Jones, and Albert Jones.

---

[210] [This Lidia's w. is in *ECC WB II (1791-1904)* /261 dated 10 Oct 1773. It was pr. 28 Oct 1773.]
[211] [20 Oct 1809 in Mecklenburg Co.,
 VA (*VA, Compiled Marriages,* 1740-1850; Provo, UT
[212] [*US Find A Grave* shows dates as Apr 1790-4 May 1856 and the bu in Meck Co.)
[213] *Prestwould Chapter DAR, M. Recs 1811-1853* Meckl Co. (Wm J. Patillo) m. bond 20 Jan 1812
[214] *Prestwould Chapter DAR, Marriage Recs 1811-1853* Meckl Co. (Alex. Field) 24 Jun 1817. Sec. JJ

b) James B Jones & Judith B Hall had Beverley Jones, **James Alfred** Jones (b 1820) who m. Mary Lyon in 1858, Col. Robt Tingnall Jones, and Edward Little John Jones.
   c) James Alfred Jones & Mary Lyon had **Mary Morni** [?] Jones who m. Judge Gardner Tyler (b 1846).
      d)Mary Morni. & Gardner had Mary Lyon Tyler (1895), **Margarett** Tyler (1897) who m. Stephen F Chadwick, David – Tyler, James Alfred Tyler, and John Tyler.
         e)Stephen Chadwick & Margarett had child: Mary Lyon Chadwick

b)Dr. Tingnall Jones & Martha REG had **Dr. William H.** Jones who m. – Raines, **Martha** Jones who m. [1] Victor Eppes [215] and [2] Thomas Eppes, and **Harriet** Jones who m – Morton.
   c)Dr. William H. Jones & -- Raines had Anna Jones
   c)Martha Jones & Victor Eppes had Dr. Victor Eppes who m. – Hall.
   c)Martha Jones & Thomas Eppes had Rosa Eppes who m. Mason Anderson.
   c)Harriet & -- Morton had Tingnall J. Morton, Martha M. Morton, and Harriet B. Morton.

b)Martha Jones & William Pattillo had James A. Pattillo (1812-94) who m. Frances Susan Smith
   c) James A. Pattillo & Frances Susan Smith (b 1816) had James G. Pattillo (1830) who m. Jennie A. Rowland (1863-1922), Fannie (1848-1901), and **Susan** Pattrillo who m. George W. Smith (1858-1905).
      d) James G. Pattillo & Jennie A. Rowland had **James A.** Pattillo (b 1886) who m. Annette Stilwell, Annie Sue Pattillo (b 1879), Rewl— Dale Pattillo who m. Selmo Taylor, MaryJ. Pattillo (b 1893) who m. – Howell, and Stewart Pattillo (b 1902).
         e) James A. & Annette Stilwell had Virginia Pattillo, Annette S. Pattillo, and Sue -- Pattillo

b)Frances Jones & -- Feild had William Field, Alexander Field, Mary Field, Ellen Field, and Osmond Field.

a)Vinkler Jones (son of Matthew IV) & Elizabeth Armistead had Westwood A[Armistead] Jones who m. Delia Jones, had **John** Jones who m. Judith Booth in 1807, **Francis** Jones m. Ann Booth in 1799, William Jones, Mary Jones who m. – Harris, Nancy Jones who m. Harper Booth in 1800, and Elizabeth Jones who m. – Burrow.
   b)Westwood A. Jones & Delia Jones had Penny Jones who m. Richard Smith, Elizabeth Jones who m. Wm. Leathers, Vinkler Jones who m. Ann Vinkler, **Tingnall** Jones (1790-1850) who m. Emily High in 1825 (b. 23 Jul 1825 Wake NC, m. TJ 25 Jan 1825 Wake Co. NC, d. 2 Jun 1864 Bastrop Co. TX][216],

---

[215] *Prestwould Chapter DAR, Marriage Recs 1811-1853 Meckl* Co. The fa of Martha M. was TJ, who gave consent. Sec. was William Jones]
[216] [*LDS Family History Library*]

Nancy Jones who m. Wm. Allen, Margaret Jones who m. James A Waddell, Ann Marie Jones who m. Augustus Hunter, Mary M. Jones who m. Thomas A Scarborough, Francis Jones, and Jack Maria [='**Penny**' – AAW].

[c) (AAW): Penny Jones m. __Smith; ch Mary who m. __Morehead.]
c)Tingnall Jones [1790-1850] & Emily High had John P Jones [1828-],and Vinkler Jones [1826-)].

b) John Jones & Judith Booth had **Caroline** Jones, and **Vinkler** Jones who m. Sam [?] Birdsong in 1829.[217]

b) Francis Jones & Ann Booth had **Minerva T**. Jones Harris (1788-) in 1821, Judith Jones who m. Meredith in 1817, **Rebecca A. C**. Jones who m. John J. Simmons in 1828, Lucy Jones, **Thomas Booth** Jones (1809-1867 who m. Minerva R. A. Booth in 1840, **Francis** Jones (d 1881) who m. Antoinette Liles (1831-63) in 1849, Herbert Jones., William Jones, **James** Joneswho m. Matilda Kernachan.

c)Benjamin Harris & Minerva T. Jones had William N—Harris (1822-1822), **Mary A. E**. Harris (1823-69) who m. Dr. W. C. Cross (1815-80) in 1841, Amanda (1826-1829), **Benjamin R**. Cross (1828-70) who m. Sallie Alexander (1832-96) in 1894, and **Minerva** Harris (1835-67) who m. Dr. D.C. Kelly.

d)Mary A.E. Harris & Dr. W. C. Cross had Minerva T. Cross (1842-78), Mary L. Cross (1845-53), **Amanda R**. (1846-1922) who m. Thomas Lile (1835-83) [below that in lighter ink "1848-99"], William Pitt Cross (1849-58), Ellen Cross, **Benjamin Jesse** Cross (1853-) who m. Mary. Alexander (1861) in 1883, William **Cyprion** Cross (1856-1911) who m. [first?] Arabella Prince in 1878, and [2] Lyda Jennings (1875-1931) in 1894, and Mary Baird Cross (1860-63).

e) Thomas Lile & Amanda R. Cross had Mary L. Lile (1872-75), Ellen Lile (1876-77), Minerva Lile (1875-75), William Cross Lile (1882-3), and **Mannie** L. Lile (b 1886) who m. Herbert C. Harris (1885) in 190[5]

f) Mannie L. & Herbert C. Harris had **Martha**, William Lile Harris (1909), and Herbert C. Harris Jr. (1915).

g)Martha R. & Karl had Karl A. Waltersdorf Jr (b 1930).

e)Benjamin Jesse Cross & Mary E. Alexander had **James Lile** Cross (1884) who m. Mary Hurst (1876) in 1908, **Benjamin H**. Cross (1885-1929) who m. Pearl Jackson (1892-) in 1910, **Mary Ann**Cross (1897-) who m. William Alex Malone (1875-), Adam S. (1889-) Mattie L. (1891-), Elizabeth **A**. Cross (1896-) who m. William DeRoy Brotherton (1893-) in 1920, William Cyprian Cross, Robert K. (1899) who m. Edith Montgomery in 1928, and **Rebecca** (1901-) who m. George V Welch.

f) James Lile & Mary had BenjaminJ. Cross (1904-09),

---

[217] *Wake Co. M. Bonds* show a Vinkler Jones m. to Euny Rogers 24 Nov 1823.]

James Lile Cross (1910), John D. Hurst (1912), Mary ElizabethCross (1914), and Thomas East (1916-).

f)BenjaminH. & Pearl had Mary Elizabeth Cross, James J. Cross (1912), Rebecca Nancy P. Cross (1914), Margaret F. (1916) BenjaminH. (1918), and William Cyprion (1926).

f)Mary Ann& William Alex Malone had Lois Nelson Malone (1909-),Jessie May Malone (1912-), Alice D. Malone (1914-), William Alex Malone (1916-), MaryAmie Malone (1918-), and Ben Cross Malone (1923-).

f) Elizabeth A. & William DeRoy had WilliamDeRoy Jr. (1921), Betty C. DeRoy (1925), and Frank Rice DeRoy (1931).

c)Rebecca A. C. Jones & John J. Simmons had **Rebecca** Simmons who m. JohnM. Malone, and **Ellen** Simmons who m. Robt Karnachen.

d)Rebecca Simmons & John M. Malone had Linda Malone who m. Samuel Chew, George Malone who m. Lena Kelly, Annie T. Malone who m. Fayette [?] Chew, Sallie . Malone, **Henry B.** Malone who m. Mamie Kelly, and John Nichols.

e)Henry B. & Mmie had **Sallie Booth** Malone who m. Horace Leeper,
e)**Rebecca** C. Malone who m. George Harsh, and Nancey Malone.

f)Sallie B. & Horace had Nancy E. Leeper.
f)Rebecca C. & George had Nancey B. Harsh.

d)Ellen & Robthad William Jones Karnachen who m. Jennie Jones, Robert Karnachen who m. Blanch More, and **John S.** Karnachen who m. Elva Moore.

e)Wm & Jennie had Hall Kernachan who m. Leila Bates, Bertha Kernachan who m. George Cushing, and **John** Kernachan II who m. Virginia Lusk.

f) John & Virginia had -- Kernachan and John K. III.

e) John S. & Elva had **Ellen** Kernachan who m. Joe Davis **Carrie,** Moore Kernachan who m. Edwin Reddisen, and **Robt** Kernachan who m. Willie Vent--.

f)Ellen & Joe had Elva M. Davis, Charlotte Davis and Joe Robt Davis (1929).
f)Carrie & Edwin had John K. Reddisen.
)Robt & Willie had Ellen Kernachan Vent--.

c) Thomas Booth Jones & Minerva R.A. had **Maria** Jones who m. – Linden, James Jones, Francis Jones and **Thomas** Ruben Jones who m. Callie Stout.

d)Maria & -- Linden had Ella Linden who m. Joe Houston, and Mollie Linden who m. – Mayfield.

c) Francis Jones & Antoinette Liles had Americus Jones who m. Col. Abanathy, DuAnn Jones and **Antoinette L V** Jones (d 1884) m. Dr. Judson Crenshaw.

d)Antoinette L V & Dr. Judson had Mary Crenshaw who m. --.
e)Mary & -- had [dau] who m. Jack Pride.

c) James Jones & Matilda Kernachen had Annie Jones [above that is written Stacey W. Allen] who m. [1] – Norris and [2] – Burgess.

d)Annie & -- Burgess had Annie C. Burgess who m. – Pomeray

105

a)Margaret Jones & John Thompson had Mary Shorr Thompson, and Elizabeth Thompson.

a) Elizabeth Jones & John Armistead had **John** Armistead who m. Elizabeth Royster, Starkey Armistead (w 1775)[218] who m. Mary --, and **Robert** Armistead (w 1792) who m. Ann -- .

    b) John & Elizabeth had Fabian Armistead.

    b)Robert & Ann had William Armistead & Elizabeth Armistead.

3. Matthew Jones m. Martha Harwood. Their sons were Matthew W. Jones (III), **Francis** Jones (W 1755 Edgecombe Co. NC) who m. Mary – [off page edge of copy], and Capt. **Harwood Jones** (1704-71) who m. Mary Chisman (b. 1723) in 1744.

    a) Francis Jones & Mary Ridley had [13 chen, 6 boys and 7 girls:] Judith Jones who m. Cpt Wilson, Mary Jones who m. Col. John Cullers, Lucy Jones who m. Cpt Brown, Bette Day Jones, Lydia Jones who m. Drury Mims, Jemima Jones, Ridley Jones, Francis who m. Frances Yancey, Matthew Jones, **John** Jones who m. Mary Cain, **Col. Tingnall** (1735-1807) who m. Penelope Cain (d.1826) in 1813[?], **Nathaniel** Jones (I) (d. 1810) who m. Ann Snickers, and **Albridgton** Jones (d. 1788) who m. – Hardy.

    b) Lydia & Drury had Tignal, Matthew Britton, Ridley, John & Lydia[219]

    b) John Jones & Mary Cain had Wiley Jones who m. Penny Jones, Samuel Jones, Lydia Ann Jones who m. John Kimb[erly], Mary Jones, and James Cain Jones who m. – Jeff[reys

    b)Col. Tingnall & Penelope had Francis Jones (d. 1844), Fanning, **Redding** (d 1816) who m. Martha Bustin, **Penelope** Jones who m. Duncan Stewart, Mary Jones who m. Charles Stewart, **Delia**[220] who m. Westwood A. Jones John C. Jones (d. 1818 [1808]), Elizabeth Jones who m. first – [Charles] Briggs and second Absalom Alston, and **Tingnall** Jones (1766-1807) who m. Peggy --.

    c)Redding & Martha had **Dr. John Ridley Jones** who m. Martha Lane, and **Tingnall** (1811-1887) who m. Susan King in 1835.

---

[218] [Starkey's w. is in *ECC WB I /276*]

[219] [This Lydia might have been the mother of the 'Redden' (or 'Reddin') Jones, orphaned infant, as she is mentioned in a Bertie Co., NC bond of 13 May 1816. Another 'Reddin" Jones, dec'd, is named in a *Craven Co., NC,* document of May 1846—pet. by his widow, Chloe. Reddin's fa had d. intestate.]

[220] [AAW: Delia Jones' dau was another Mary Smith. Mary's fa was Dr. James Smith of Hillsborough (NC). Delia was dau of Frank {Francis} Jones , son of Tignal (?) and Mary Cain].

d) Dr. John Ridley Jones & Martha had **Thomas Grant** Jones (b. 1900) who m. Mildred Elizabeth Bass (1846-79). [AAW
e) Thomas Grant & Mildred had Martha Jones who m. J.J. Patterson, John ReddingJ ones who m. Mary Wilson, Madere Jones, Thomas Grant Jones Jr., and **Leila** Jones who m. Judge Charles Wellborn (b 1867).
f)Leila & Judge Charles had Olin Wellborn (1896), Mildred Wellborn (1899) who m. George Nathaniel Whiting in 1917, Charles Wellborn Jr. (1901), and Dorothy Lillian Wellborn (1903).
c)Penelope & Duncan had Tingnall Stewart.
c)Mary & Charles Stewart had Tingnall Stewart.
d)Tingnall & Susan King had **Hartwell K. Jones** (1840—1916) who m. Mary Frances Bracher (b 1846) in 1867.
e)Hartwell & Mary Frances had **Anne** A. Jones (b 1868) who m. James Blake Kennard (b 1801), and Susan Jones who m . –Dilworth.
f)Anne A. & James Blake had Hartwell S. Kennard (b 1803) who m. Eleanor Wurzbeck in 1920.
g)Hartwell & Eleanor had Hartwell Wurzbeck and **Emily Ann Wurzbeck** [?].
c)Tingnall & Peggy had **Frances** Jones (1791-1871) who m. Christopher Berber (1779-183?).
d)Frances **& Christopher** had **W. Gaston Berber** (1824-84) who m. Louise C. F (1840-19??).
e)W. Gaston & Louise had **Cadia** Berber who m. John cott --.
b)Nathaniel & Ann Snickers had Albridgton Jones who m. Cadie Barts, **Nathaniel Jones** (1758-1828) [17 May 1828; this NJ is called 'Crabtree Jones' in some sources] who m. first Elizabeth Perry and 1766-1840) who m. first Ann Jones, second Grizeal Kimbrough (d 1774) [7 Dec 17_9_4] in ~~1762,~~[221] **Henry** Jones (almost invisible, is 'Nancy'] and second Sallie M. Smith in 1806, **Matthew** Jones who m. Sarah Kimbrough (d. 1808) [See, item 10 FHL catalog 1697588], 1766-1840) who m. first Ann Jones, second Grizeal Kimbrough (d 1774) [7 Dec 1794] in 1762,[222] Henry Jones (almost invisible, is 'Nancy'] and second Sallie M. Smith in 1806, Matthew Jones who m. Sarah Kimbrough (d. 1808) [See, item 10 FHL catalog 1697588], **Margaret** Jones who m. James Kimbrough, **Hasea Jones** who m. William Barbee, **Anne** Jones who m __ Wooten, **Polly** Jones who m. first __Pope and second Milton Paxton, Ridley Jones, and Richard Jones

---

[221] [The m. of NJ & Grizeal was 16 May 17_82_{*Bible of Nath'l J. 1758-1915*}. The M. bond was 11 May 1782 {*Wake Co. M. Bonds*}. He was b. 27 Oct, 1758 m. "the 2nd time Betsy Perry" 11 Apr 1797' – Bible.]

[222] [The m. of NJ & Grizeal was 16 May 17_82_{*Bible of Nath'l J. 1758-1915*}. The M. bond was 11 May 1782 {*Wake Co. M. Bonds*}. He was b. 27 Oct, 1758 m. "the 2nd time Betsy Perry" 11 Apr 1797' – Bible.]

[We insert in brackets entries from the family Bible, 'Bible of Nath'l Jones 1758-1915.'][223]

c)Nathaniel & Grizeal had: **Kimbrough** Jones (1783-1866)[224] who m.
(1) Mrs. **Ann Massenburg** in 1813 [This Ann was probably the Nancy who d. 13 Apr 1815; ch dyng].
(2) **Mary P. Hogan** [m. 10 May 1821, d. 18 Jun 1833} chen: John (24 Jun 1814-31 May 1815), William
(-c1861). Nat[haniel][225] (- 1860), William Hogan (4 Mar 1826-5 May 1865)].
(3) **Mary Webb Warren**, [m. 19 Sep 1837, d. 25 Mar 1891

[Other chen of the m. of Nathl & Grizeal were: **Martha (Patsy) Jones** (1784-) [-20 Jul 1836, who m. (1) Daniel C. Edwards [20 Apr 1806 & (2) Rev. Henry Warren in the fall of 1819; he d. 20 Dec 1850; **Ann (Nancy) Jones** (9 Feb 1788-30 Jun 1856) who m. Gen. Thos D. King 12 Sep 1827. He d. 24 Feb 1854].

[The chen of m. (3) of Kimbrough Jones (i.e. to Mary Webb Warren) were **Martha Elizabeth (Patsy) Jones, Ann [Mary Ann Jones** (above her name, almost invisible, is 'Nancy' – [she is called 'Nancy' (23 Nov 1839- 30 Jun 1856)], who m. ___1854,].
[Henry W{arren} Jones m. Nancy __ 3 Feb 1813[226] d. 7 Sep 1891].
 d)Kimbrough & Mary P. had John Allen Jones [18 Jun 1833-13 Oct 1844][221], Nath'l Jones (d. 20 Apr 1860 William **Hogan** Jones [b. 4 Mar 1826] who m. [13 Sep 1853] Sarah E. Smith.
 d)Kimbrough & Mary Webb had Mary Jones who m, WK Davis, Kimbrough Jones who m. Mary Green,[227] ......
  e)Wm & Sarah had Mary H. Jones , **Mildred H.** Jones who . J. H. Wissler, Kimbrough Jones [d. 15 Feb 1863],[228] and **Sallie** Jones who m. Frank Borden.
   f)Mildred Jones & J.H. Wissler had Christian Wissler, and Sarah Wissler
    f)Sallie & Frank had Frank Borden (1888) who m. Margaret Gold in 1925, Arnold Borden(1889), **Mildred** Borden (1891) who m. Robt. Hanes in 1917, Julia Borden (1892) who m. Fitzhugh Lee [in 1910?], Edwin Borden, and Sarah Borden (1894) who m. Powell B. Cobb in 1926.

---

[223] [*This Bible rec. is in the Family Records Collection of the NC State Archives.* It is often too faint to read and contains some items which seem contradictory or confusing or for which no connections are evident, e.g. ' John Junior Jones, son of Kinde Douglas (Jones?) & Nancy Jones,' ' John Jones d. 31 May 1816.'
[224] [Kim Jones, son of NJ & Grizeal, (26 Apr 1783-30 Mar 1866) {*Bible of Nath'l J. 1758-1915*}.] Another source is *Wake V*/281+ citing several chen
[225] Info re the chen of ms. 1 & 2 provided by AAW.
[226] *NC Co. Ms.*/277]
[227] [See *Crabtree Jones Papers* re Mary Green.
[228] **Nathl Jones** Bible at LVA

g)Mildred & Robt. Hanes had Frank Hanes, & Sarah Hanes d. 7 Sep 1891 (or 1 Jun 1893?], Pattie Jones who m. Willis Whitaker [Was Pattie the Martha Elizabeth b. 10 Nov 1844?], **Penelope** Jones [b. 8 Jun 1846] who m. [23 Dec 1863] Tom [W.] Davis [and might have m. (2) a Mr. Smith; a Penelope Smith is listed as b. into this fam 8 Jun 1846], and [**Emily**] **Meta Jones** [b. 1 Aug 1855] who m. Needham [P.] Jones [6 Jun 1876

e)Kimbrough & **Mary Green** had Bryan K. Jones, Elizabeth Jones who m. Stacey W. Allen, Peter H—Jones, James Jones, Mary K. Jones, Wm. K. Jones [b. 4 Mar 1828], and [written in] James. Edward Kimbrough.

e)Penelope & Tom had Mary W. Davis who m. Irwin Holt, Archibald Davis, Nina Davis who m. --Plummer, Pattie Davis who m. Roy Jackson, Wm. K. Davis, John N. Davis, Thomas W. Davis, Kimbrough Davis, Penelope Davis, Rebie Davis,and Lola Davis.

e)Needham & Meta had Kimbrough Jones and Elizabeth Jones who m. John Pearson, [and Nancy Warren Jones d.14 Sep.1887].

c)Henry & Ann had Sidney Jones who m. Elizabeth Merritt, Amelia Jones who m. Wilson Whitaker, Nathaniel, **Rufus** Jones who m. Sarah Merritt, and Adolphus Jones who m. Frances Hooker.

d)Rufus & Sarah had Lily Jones, Sidney Jones, Lula Jones who m. T.K. Mason, and Leonidas Jones

c) Matthew & Sarah Kimbrough had **Nat. K**. Jones (1800-62) who m. first Lucy Norment and second Caroline Jane Jones, **Kimbrough** Jones who m. Susan, **Daniel** Jones who m. Ann Raegan, **Mary** Jones who m. __ Hancock and **Ann** Snickers Jones who m. William Harper.

d)Nat. K. Jones. & Lucy had Lucy Jones who m. C D McSwain, and Jamie Jones who m. N S Grew.

d) Nat. K. Jones & Caroline had Senator **James K[im]. Jones I** (1839- 1908) who m. Sue R. Eaton.

e)Senator James & Sue had Steve Carrigan who m. Sue Sumerville, and Nat. Jones.

f)Nora and Steve had **Steve Carrigan Jr** who m. Mary Delia Peine, **Lillian** Carrigan who m. Ralph Routon, and Mary Kim Carrigan who m. TS McDoritt.

g)Steve & Mary had Mary Delia Carrigan.

g}Lilliam & Ralph had William Ralph Routon, and Frances Lenora Routon.

f)the Jones boy who m. Sue Sumerville had Nat. Jones, **James K.** Jones II who m. first Cora Benson

and second Annette Taylor, and Mary Jones who m. Frank Plant.
    g) James K. & Cora had Margaret Jones, and James K. III.
    g) James K. & Annette had Elizabeth Jones who m. Lt. Henry Slocum.
        h) Elizabeth & Lt. Henry had Anne Taylor Slocum.
d)Kimbrough & Susan had Calvin Jones, Mary who m. first Duff – and second – Trotter, and Anne Jones who m. first – Minor and second – Harris.
d)Daniel Jones & Ann Raegan had Nat K. Jones who m. Millar [?] Gibson, Harper Jones, Elina Jones, Elvin Jones, Henry Jones, William Jones, Dan Jones who m. Julie Williams, Ann Marie Jones, and **Mae** Jones who m. – Power.
    e)Dan & Julie had Sarah Ruth Jones who m. Alvin Stevens.
    e)Mae & -- Power had Roberta Power,,,Mary Kim. Power, Ann Power, and Ruth Power.
    d)Mary & -- Hancock had Sidney Hancock, Ed. Hancock, [boy] Hancock who m. Norma Webber, and [unnamed child] who m. – Hill. Ann Snickers Jones & William Harper had James s Harper, **William**
    Harper who m. Nobie Blackburn, Albert Harper, **Sallie** Harper who m. Norbun Young, and Anne Harper who m. – Todd.
    e) William Harper & Nobie had Raleigh B. Harper, and **Mary Kim** Harper who m. C W Black.
        f) Mary Kim & CW had CW Black Jr.
    e)Sallie Harper & Norbun Young had Kimbrough Young, **Sallie** Young who m. John McNeil, Albert Young, Paul Young, Annie who m. – Linebough, and Ruth Young who m. – Rogers.
        f)Sallie Young & John McNeil had Mildred McNeil, John McNeil, William McNeil, and Nora McNeil.
    e)Anne Harper and – Todd had Elizabeth Todd, Emma Todd, and Walter Todd
c)Margaret Jones & James Kimbrough had Goldman Kimbrough, Patsy Kimbrough, Nathaniel Kimbrough (1782-1833), and Willis Kimbrough (d 1832).
c)Anna Jones & -- Wooten had Anna Wooten,and Benjamin Wooten.
c)Polly Jones & -- Paxton had Milton Paxton.

Appendix 4, CT & WP

There was a separation of families: 'White Plains' (WP) or 'Crabtree' (CT). These designations had to do with the locations of their seats of residence.

One location was at Crabtree Creek and the other at White Plains, both in NC. The WP Jones line apparently began with an Evan Jones (a name that was fairly plentiful), but the distinction seems less than absolute.[230] For us, the only difference I've seen is that there were two Nathaniel Joneses, WP and CT, at the same time in Wake Co. The two branches intermarried.

info from Mrs. Whitaker: In tree form the first m. of NJ looks like this:
Nathaniel Jones

Sarah Elizabeth ('[Betsy')[231]	Nancy	Mary	Seth Blanchard Jones
			(-Aug 1860)
m. __Alston	m. __Palmer		
daus Mary &	3 sons (1 m.),		
Nancy m. John	1 grandson		
& Thomas			
deGraffenreid;			
1 son had 1 dau.			
(See 'S. Gentry' below)			

Ann Elizabeth   Alpheus   Charity   Mrs. Green   Mrs. Crudup   Seth Blanchard Jones[232]
  | (---all d. bef. 1895 except Mrs. Crudup, who was living in 1883---)
  m. __Montague
_____|_____
(unnamed chen)

[The *NC Estate Files* for Wake Co. give us some further info on the family of **Seth Blanchard Jones, Sr.** (There was a son of the same name, so we must distinguish them with Seth Sr. and Seth Jr.)[233]. Sr. was a rich man. He d. testate in 1866 (even though the index says '1860'), and his w. was pr. 29

---

[230] **Mrs. Amelia Ann Whitaker** (hereafter 'AAW') says (at the end of her letters to **Susie Gentry** [quoted in full by McSwain and located in the 'round file' at the NC Library]): 'My great grfa [**Nathaniel Jones**, ... I suppose left relations in VA.' She also speaks of **Col. Tignal Jones** as her 'great uncle' and also says in one place that her grandfather was WP and in another that he was CT, so there doesn't appear to have been a lot of clarity in the WP/CT distinction.

[231] Unless this **Betsy Alston** was another person, AAW confused her with Betsy Alston, the dau -in-l of Col. Tignal Jones. That Betsy m. 1st **Charles Briggs.**

[232] Mrs. Whitaker's letter says there were 3 sons but she names only 2, Alpheus & Seth.

[233] Also there was later a Seth A. Jones according to the *NC Soldiers and Widows Pension Applications, 1885-1953.* This man was b. c1845 and d. aft.19 Jul 1904. He enlisted in 1862 (making his age then c17) was wounded in 1864 (age c19) and was paralyzed as a result. The rec. shows that he applied also for admission to the Home for Disabled in Raleigh, and that he was 'now unmarried.'

Sept 1866 in Wake Co., NC. His wife was **Sally K.** Son **'Seth Blanchard Jones' [Jr.]** (so indexed in the Estate Files) d. c1879, also testate. The executors of Sr. were both m. to Sr's daughters: **Columbia** (living in 1883) m. **Dr. Edw. A. Crudup,** and **Anna Elizabeth** m. **Dr. Henry W. Montague.** Dr. Crudup d. in Apr 1876. He also, had a son of the same name, who was ex. for Seth, Jr. in 1879. Dau **Charity** m. **Wm. A. Whitfield.** Dau **Susan Sarah** m. **Wm W. Green.** A son or son-in-law of Sr. seems to have been **Alston A.**, but the records in one place say ' **John Alston**' and in another place the reference is to 'the Alston A. Jones chen' as heirs to the estate of Seth, Sr. The chen of **Alpheus** were **Needham P.,**[234] **Alfred,** and **Nannie** (sp?} **P.** Alpheus d. bef. 8 Apr 1879. Some of the chen of Seth, Sr. moved to other states, but the info is unclear about which persons went where. Some went to Shelly, MS (evidently the **Whitfields**), and some to Kosse [sp?], Lewiston [sp?] Co., TX. There is also mention of some having gone to TN.

AAW says 'Grfa' **Nathaniel**'s 2nd wife was **Rachael Perry.** Chen: **Joel, Alfred, Burwell, Timothy, Wesley, Mrs. Amelia Pulliam, Mrs. Temperance Whitaker** (m. **Col. Willis Whitaker** [who fought in war of 1812], a widower wi one son **Wilson Whitaker** {see above}). 'Aunt Temperance' had 4 sons: The 2 named were **Burwell** (whose daus were **Mrs. Black** and **Mrs. Hill**); **Wesley** m. **Miss Courts** and they had 2 daus and 2 sons, **Alfred and George.**
Grapically:

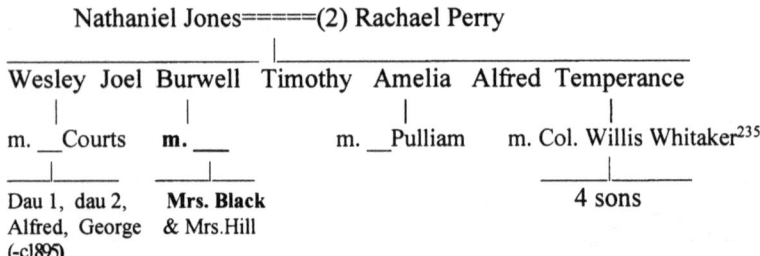

A **Burwell P. Jones** appears in the *NC Estate Files* for Wake Co. for 1835. His wife was **Mary P.** He d. intestate in 1835 & had chen **Alfred, Archibald, Louisa E., Rachel P., Helen, Francis,** and **Elaine. Louisa** m. **Jacob G. Wheeler.** The files mention Seth Jones as providing board for the boys, Alfred & Archibald, paid 13 Jan 1838. Mentions H[elen?]. & **Mary**

---

[234] Needham P. d. in Wake Co. in 1907 [NC Est Files] which list [chen?] Mrs. Nannie P. Jones, Miss Lizzie P. Jones, and Miss Lilian Crudup.
[235] AAW: His son, Wilson Whitaker, m. AAW.

Palmer Jones for girls' board Jan 1840. **Alston A. Jones** adm estate of Alfred Jul 1846. Lands adj **Kim. Jones** et al. Mentions land of **Henry Jones.** NC m. bonds & the recs of Wake Co. show a m. **Burwell P. Jones** to **Franci[e]s T. Hunter** on 7 Dec 1816 and a m. Burwell Jones to Decy Pope on 8 Nov 1817. (The latter might be a misspelling of 'Burnell' Jones.. **John Jones** is also bonded by the Hunter m. bond.

Appendix 5:

Maps of the MJH and site

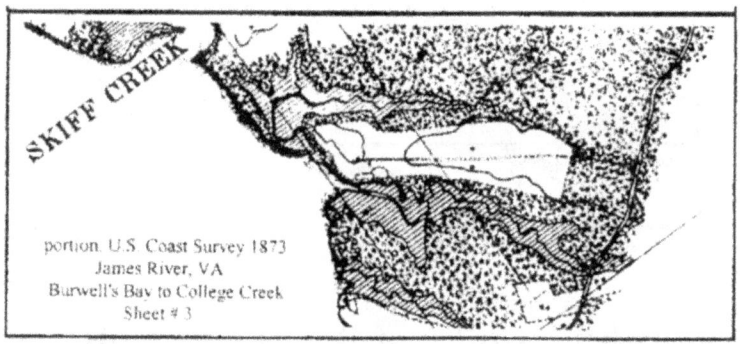

portion U.S. Coast Survey 1873
James River, VA
Burwell's Bay to College Creek
Sheet # 3

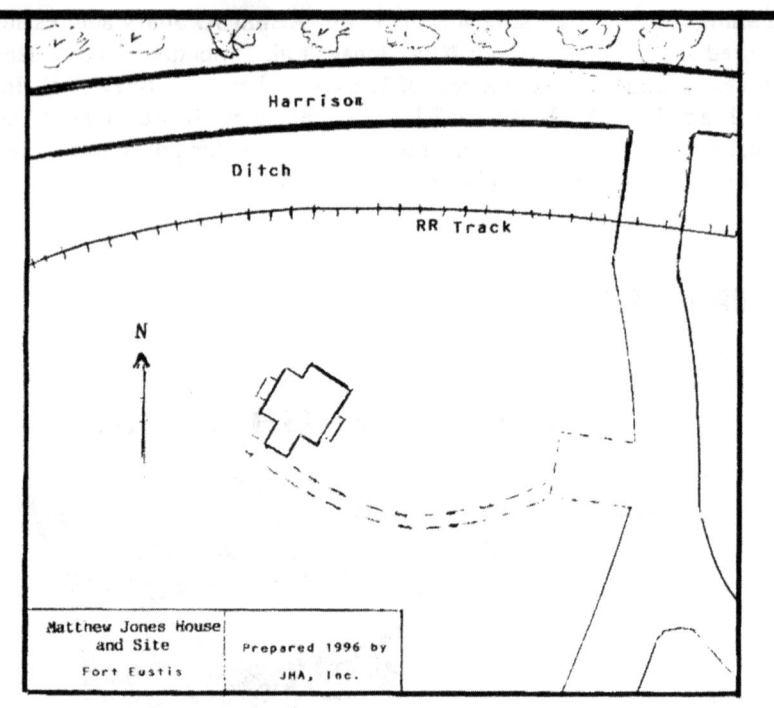

Bibliography of Books and Collections
(does not include court records or most journal issues)

Bell, Landon C., *Charles Parish, York County, VA;* Baltimore, Clearfield, 1999

Bentley, *Ms of Wake Co. 1770-1868,* Baltimore, Gen. Pub. Co., 1983

Bishop Meade, *Old Churches, Ministers and Families*

Bockstruck, *VA's Colonial Soldiers*, Baltimore, Gen. Pub. Co., 1988

Boddie, John Bennet, *Southside VA Families,* Baltimore, Gen. Pub. Co., 1964

Boddie, John Bennet, *Hist. Southern Families;* self pub.,

Boddie, John Bennet, *Seventeenth Century Isle of Wight*, reprint: Baltimore, Gen. Pub. Co.

Brewer, Mary M., *York County VA, Deeds, Orders, Wills, 1698-1700*; Berwyn Heights, Heritage, 2019

Broughton, *NC M. and D. 1799-1825*; v.2 1826-1845; Baltimore, Gen. Pub. Co.

Brydon, George MacLaren, *Dictionary of Virginia Biography*

Cain, *Provincial Congress*

Cain, *Colonial Recs of NC*

Chamberlain, *History of Wake Co.;* Raleigh, Edwards and Broughton, 1922

Chapman, *Wills and Admins. of Southampton and of Isle of Wight Counties*. Reprint Gen. Pub. Co., Baltimore, c1980

Chapman, *Isle of Wight Co. Marriages 1628-1899*, Reprint Gen. Pub. Co., Baltimore, 1976

Cognets, *Eng. Duplicates of Lost VA Recs*; Huntsville, AL, 1958, Reprint Gen. Pub. Co., Baltimore, 1981

Crabtree Jones Papers (at NC State Library)

Crozier, *VA Colonial Militia 1651-1776*, Baltimore, Gen. Pub. Co., 1982

Crozier, *Early VA Ms*; (Vol. IV of VA Colonial Recs.), Gen. Pub. Co., Baltimore, 1982

Daughters of American Colonists

Davis, *Surry Co. Recs. 1652-1684*; Reprint Gen. Pub. Co., Baltimore, 1980

Dodd, *NC Ms., Early to 1800*; Precision Indexing Publishers, SLC

Davis, Camilla Webb, *unpublished chart of the descendants of Matthew Jones of Mulberry Island*. [In Dunn, *Warwick County, Virginia, The 1643 Church on Baker's Neck and the Genealogy of Neighbor Matthew Jones*, Baltimore, MD: Clearfield, 2019]

Dorman, *York County Deeds*

Dunn, F. Richard, *A History of the Briggs and Phillips Families and Related Lines*; self 2008

Dunn, F. Richard, *Warwick County, Virginia, Colonial Court Records in Transcription*, Baltimore, Clearfield, 3rd ed. 2008, 675 pages.

Dunn, F. Richard, *Supplement* to *Warwick County, Virginia, Colonial Court Records in Transcription*, Baltimore, Clearfield, 3rd ed. 2016

Dunn, F. Richard, *Warwick County, Virginia, Court Records in Transcription 1782-1851*, Baltimore, Clearfield, 2nd ed. 2018

Dunn, F. Richard, *Warwick County, Virginia, The 1643 Church on Baker's Neck and the Genealogy of Neighbor Matthew Jones*, Baltimore, Clearfield, 2019

Duvall, *York County, VA, Wills, Deeds & Orders 1657-1659*

Eckenrode, *List of Colonial Soldiers of VA*, Baltimore, Gen. Pub. Co., 1980

Elliott, *Early Wills [Mecklenburg Co., VA], 1765-1800*

Fleet, *VA Colonial Abstracts;* reprint: Baltimore, Gen. Pub. Co.

Fothergill & Naugle, *VA Taxpayers 1782-87*; Baltimore, Gen. Pub. Co., 1978

Fulham Papers (Colonial FP XII f78) – survey report

Gardener, Lyon, *Encyclopedia of Virginia Biography*, Vols I-II. New York: Lewis Historical Publishing Company, Archive.org

Gill, *Apprentices of VA 1623-1800,* Salt Lake City, Ancestry.

Grimes, *Abstracts of NC Wills;* Baltimore, Gen. Pub. Co., 1980

Hathaway, *NC Hist. and Gen. Reg.*

Hatch, **The First 17 Years: VA 1607-1624**; Charlottesville, Univ. Press, 1957

Haun, *Wake Co., NC, Land Entries 1778-1840,* Durham, NC, Haun, 1980

Heitman, *Hist. Reg. of Officers of the Continental Army during the War of the Rev. Apr 1775-Dec 1883*; Baltimore, Gen. Pub. Co., 1973

Henning, *Statutes at Large,* Charlottesville, Univ. Press of VA

Holcomb, **Ms. of Wake Co., NC 1770-1868**; Baltimore, Gen. Pub. Co., 1983

Holcomb, *Meck'burg Co., NC. Abstracts of Early Ws. 1763-1768*

Jones House Association Inc., *Notes-- (1994-2002)* Quarterly journal of the JHA (found at the Library of VA and elsewhere)

Knorr, *Marriage Bonds and Ministers' Returns of Southampton County, VA, 1750-1810;* Pine Bluff, AR

Ludlum, David M., *Early American Hurricanes*

Mason, George Carrington, *'Colonial Churches in War. and Eliz. City Cos.'* and other articles in VMBH

McGhan & Bentley, comps.,   1981 Gen Pub Co., Baltimore

McIlwaine, *Executive Journals of the Council of Colonial VA*

McSwain, *Some Descendants of Francis Albridgeton (1609-17--)/ Mathew Jones / Francis Albridgton Jones;* McSwain, Jones & Grissom, printer; Macon, GA, , 1984 [to be found at LVA, LDS library in Salt Lake City (shelf no. 929.273 Al 15m) and elsewhere]

Mitchell, **NC Wills 1665-1900. A Testator Index**; Raleigh, NC, 1987

Nottingham, *The M. License Bonds of Meck'burg Co., VA from 1765 to 1810;* Onancock, VA; self, 1928.

Nugent, *Cavaliers and Pioneers...1623-1732*, 3 vols., (reprint Baltimore, Genealogical Publishing Company, 1979)

National Genealogical Society, *Index of Revolutionary War Pensions in the Nat'l Archives...*

Olds, *Abstracts of NC Ws.;* Baltimore, Genealogical Publishing Company, 1978

Opperman, Anthony, *Phase 1 Archaeology Study for Ft. Eustis...*Mid-Atlantic Archaeological Research Associates, Williamsburg 1968

Ratcliff, *NC Taxpayers 1679-1790*; Baltimore, Genealogical Publishing Company, 1987

Ridgell, Col., **unpublished report on MJA and Jones family**. Historian's Office at Ft. Eustis

Saffel, ***Recs of the Rev. War***; *1894* original by Gen. Pub. Co., Baltimore, 1969

Schreiner-Yantis, ***1787 Personal Tax List;*** *Springfield, VA, Gen, Bks in Print, 1987*

Swem, ***VA Historical Index;*** *Gloucester, Mass., Peter Smith, 1965*

Tarter, Brent, **"*The Church of England in Colonial VA*"** in 112VMBH/4/349

Torrence, ***The Ed. Pleasants Valentine Papers***; Baltimore, Genealogical Publishing Company, 1979

Trudell, Clyde F., ***Colonial Yorktown***, 1971

Tyler Collection, Canterbury, Kent, England

Upton, Dell, ***Holy Things and Profane, The Anglican Parish Church in Virginia***; New Haven, Yale U. Press

U of NC, Wilson Lib., ***NC Collection: newspaper notices from the 'Star' 1810-1826***

U.S. Find a Grave

VA Genealogical Society, ***VA Rev. War State Pensions***

Virkus, ***Compendium of Amer. Genealogies;*** Baltimore, Genealogical Publishing Company, 1925-1968

Vollertson, ***Who Was Who ...***, Ft. Eustis Hist. and Arch. Society

Watkins, ***York County Deeds & Orders*** (As some of the record books at York Co. were not indexed, Mr. Watkins undertook to index at least one of them)

Wheeler, ***Hist of NC***

White, ***Genealogical Abstracts of Revolutionary Pensions Filed***

William & Mary Center for Archaeological Research, ***A Preservation Plan for the Matthew Jones House, Ft. Eustis***, *VA, Technical Report Series Nr. 3*; The Society of the Alumni, College of Wm and Mary.

SWilson, *Catalog of Rev, Soldiers & Sailors of the Comm. of VA* ...Baltimore, So. Bk Co. 1953

Wilson Library, U of N C, *NC Collection*

Wm T.R. Saffell, *Records of the Revolutionary War 1894* original by Gen. Pub. Co., Baltimore, 1969

Wulfeck, *Ms of Some VA Residents 1607-1800*; Baltimore, Genealogical Publishing Company, 1986

Wynne, *Wake Co., NC, Abstracts of Ws....1771-1802*; Baton Rouge, Oracle Press, 1984

Name Index

Readers should use a great deal of imagination in exploring names. The names of individuals often are given variably, especially in the use of nicknames – as sometimes might be found in the following examples: Martha/Patsy, Bette/Beth/Betty/Betsy/Elizabeth, Peg/Margaret, Penny/Penelope, Mary/Pollly, Sarah/Sally, Ann/Nancy, etc. Conversely, similar names could indicate different persons. Likewise the presence or absence of a middle name might provide reference to a particular (different) person, but it might not. Likewise titles like Cpt., Col., Dr., etc. may be distinctive or not. The form used in the source is used in the text. In every case the scribe (including this author) might be unable accurately to read (or hear in census taking) the source information.

In the CWD chart only names in the main text of this book are indexed. Other names are listed by generation in the cwd text.

Thanks to Maria Sullivan for her expert work in organizing this index.

Several short extraneous messages were discovered and removed from the text after the index was finished, therefore it is possible that a few entries could be on a page adjacent to the page number shown in the index.

A

Albridgton (or Albritton, etc.)
  Elizabeth, 13, 15–17, 22, 35, 54, 57, 78, 80
  Francis, 21
  George, 16
Allen
  Mary, 22, 24
  Sarah C., 26, 34, 67
  Stacey W., 109
  William, 104
Alston
  Col. Absalom, 63, 78, 84, 106
  Elizabeth, 55
  Joseph, 55
  Joseph A., 55
Anderson
  James, 90–91
  Martha, 86, 88, 102
  Sarah, 81, 88–90
  Thomas, 88, 90
  Thomas, Jr., 88, 90
Andrews
  Henry, 15
Applewhaite
  Priscilla, 18
Applewhite
  Sarah Ann, 51
Armistead
  Edward, 46
  Elizabeth, 74–76, 87, 95, 102
  Jane, 45–46, 87, 94, 102
  John, 75, 102
  John, Jr., 91
  Moss, 46
  Westwood, 75–76
  William, 86
Asque
  John, 32
Atkins, 2
Avery, 2

B

Baker
  Benjamin, 22, 50
  Gen. Lawrence, 22, 50
Banks
  Benjamin, 62
  Ruth, 98
  Sampson, 62
Barbee
  William, 107
Barnes
  Ann, 57
  John, 57
Barts
  Cada, 52
Bass
  Mildred Elizabeth, 107
  Scion, 47
Bates
  Julia Rachel, 80
Bell
  David, 97–98
Benjamin
  Thomas, 22, 74
Bennet
  Ed, 32
Benson
  Cora, 109
Berber
  Christopher, 107
Binns
  Elizabeth, 19, 63
  Thomas, 19, 21–22
Black
  C. W., 110
  C. W., Jr., 110
Blackburn
  Mariana, 90
  Nobie, 110
Booth
  Miss, 45
  Harper, 74, 103

  Judith, 74, 103–104
  Margaret, 75
  Nancy, 74, 76
Borden
  Arnold, 108
  Edwin, 108
  Frank, 108
  Julia, 108
  Mildred, 108
  Sarah, 108
Boyd
  Richard B. Francis, 90
  Robert, 89–90, 101–102
  Sarah A., 89
Bradford
  Nathaniel, 31
Brantley
  John, 64
  Thomas, 19
Bressie
  Susannah, 95
  William, 95
Briant
  Thomas, 20
Briggs
  Charles, 77, 84, 97–98
  Elizabeth, 78
  George, 51
  John, 63
  Willis G., 82
Brown
  Capt., 41
  Dr., 19–20
Browne
  Dr., 22
  Elizabeth Ridley, 18
  Jesse, 18
  Dr. Jesse, 43
  Samuel, 43
Buckner
  Anne Timson, 69
  Nancy Simpson, 69
Burges
  Rev. Henry, 22

Burnell
  John, 75, 95
Burrow
  Mr., 103
  Elizabeth, 76
Burwell
  Carter, 24, 66, 95
  George Harrison, 96
  Lucy, 95
  Philip, 95
  Randolph, 95
  Susanna Grymes, 96
  Thomas Hugh Nelson, 96
  William, 95
Bustian
  Martha, 100, 106
  Mary, 83

C

Cain
  Elisha, 31, 87, 92, 97
  Mary, 41, 49, 106
  Penelope, 41
  Penny, 84
Calvert
  Frances, 22
  Polly, 22, 33, 51–52
Cannon
  Carl, 35
Cargill
  Elizabeth, 63
Carrigan
  Lillian, 109
  Mary Delia, 109
  Mary Kim, 109
  Steve, 109
  Steve, Jr., 109
Carter
  Dr. Lewis Robert, 95
Cary
  Richard, 23
  William, 27, 59

Chapman
   Elizabeth, 62
Childs
   Francis, 84, 94, 100
Chisman
   Eleanor, 34, 81–82
   Harwood, 80
   John, 59, 80
   Mary, 30, 40, 79–81
   William, 80
Cobb
   Powell B., 108
Crafford
   Dr. John, 67
   William, 67
Crenshaw
   Mary, 102
   Rachel, 80–82, 102
Crew
   Randall, 35
Crisp
   Mary K., 84
Crumpler
   Molly, 33
Cullers
   John, 42
   Mary, 42

D

Dangerfield
   Mr., 61
Davidson
   Sarah, 62
Davis
   Archhibald, 109
   Camilla Webb, 11
   John N., 109
   Kim, 56
   Lola, 109
   Mary W., 109
   Nina, 109
   Pattie, 109

Penelope, 109
Polly, 54, 62
Rebie, 109
Thomas, 109
Thomas W., 109
W. K., 108
William K., 109
Day
   Bette, 41, 87
   Elizabeth, 18, 22, 42
   Lydia, 102
   Thomas, 17, 32
Deberry
   Peter, 32
DeGraffenreidt
   Tscharner, 99
Dilworth
   Mr., 107
Dowell
   John, 16
Dowsing
   Mr., 60
   James, 59
   John, 23
Duncan
   Mary, 73
   Sarah, 34, 73

E

Eaton
   Sue R., 109
Edwards
   Michael, 62
Eppes
   Martha Jones, 90
   Victor, 101
   Victor M., 90

F

Field
　Frances A., 90
　Mary, 103
　Mary A., 90
Filmer
　Elizabeth, 34
　Henry, 3
Fitchett
　G. W., 8
Flood
　William, 46
Floyd
　James, 15
Foster
　Mr., 75, 95

G

Galt
　Dr. James, 60
Gentry
　Susie, 40, 100, 111
George
　Frances, 64
　Frances Servant, 17
　John, 64
Gibbons
　Lawrence, 65
Gibson
　Millar, 110
Gilliam
　William, 24
Gold
　Margaret, 108
Goodwin
　James, 59
　Matthew, 34
Goosley
　William, 24, 28
Grant
　Judge, 42, 83
　James, 83
　Martha Bustian, 41, 83
　Susie, 42
Green
　John, 34
　Mary, 108–109
Grew
　N. S., 109

H

Hancock
　Mr., 109
　Edward, 110
Hanes
　Frank, 109
　Robert, 108–109
　Sarah, 109
Harding
　David, 78
Hardy
　Mary, 41, 50
　Penny, 41, 50, 52
Harper
　Albert, 110
　Anne, 110
　James, 110
　Mary Kim, 110
　Raleigh B., 110
　Sallie, 110
　William, 109–110
Harrington
　Kitura Briggs, 82
Harris
　Mr., 110
　Mary, 76
　Richard, 75, 95
　Robert, 74
　Thomas D., 54
Harrison
　Margaret, 62
Harvey

Becky, 36
Miles, 22, 50
Col. Miles, 22
Thomas, 22, 48, 50
Harwood
Col. Edward, 60
Maj. H., 15
Maj. Humphrey, 34
Martha, 30–31, 34, 36, 39–40, 69, 79–80, 88–89, 106
Thomas, 3–4, 25
Hawkins
Frances, 95
Hay
Elizabeth Gwynn, 96
Hayes
Dr., 22, 43, 50
Dr. Barry, 43
Haynes
Laurence, 59
Hayward
Henry, 9–10, 14
High
Emily, 87, 91, 93, 103–104
Hill
William, 84
Hinton
Miss, 100
Hodges
Ann V., 76
Douglas, 76
Douglas F., 76
Hogan
Mary P., 56, 68, 108
Holt
Irwin, 109
Thomas, 20, 22
Hooker
Frances, 109
Hopkins
Mr., 101
Edmund, 90
Martha, 89

Martha C., 89–90
Hubbard, 2
Mr., 3
Cuthbert, 23
Dr. George Miles, 62
James, 34
Mary, 34, 62, 70, 73
Matthew, 28, 36
Robert, 3
Sarah, 24, 34, 73–74
Huckabee
Elizabeth, 43
Hunter
Augustus, 76, 104
Maria, 76, 104
Hurd, 2

I

Iken, 2
John, 2
Ironmonger
Martha Jones, 63

J

Jackson
Roy, 109
Jarrell
Ben, 22
Benjamin, 50
Elizabeth, 79
Jeffreys
George W., 100
Helena, 55
Nancy, 83
Peggy, 83
Johnson
Elizabeth, 75, 95
Sarah, 33
Jones
Abraham, 32, 57

Adolphus, 109
Agatha, 16–17, 20–22, 48, 50, 66
Albridgton, 1, 11, 16–24, 30, 33, 38, 40–43, 46–54, 56, 62, 66, 72, 85, 87, 95–98, 106–107
Col. Albridgton, 33
Lt. Albridgton, 49
Albridgton II, 30
Albridgton, Jr., 23
Col. Albridgton, Sr., 33
Alexander Strechen, 101
Alfred, 45, 47, 55, 112
Allen, 18, 20, 22–24, 26–29, 34, 46, 54–55, 62, 66, 71–74, 76, 104
Allen Dudley, 68
Amelia, 55
Amy, 86, 91
Ann, 17, 20–22, 29, 46, 50, 58–61, 64, 70, 76, 99–103, 106–108, 110–111
Anna, 110
Anna B., 34, 56, 95
Anne A., 107
Ann Marie, 110
Ann Snickers, 110
Ann Timson, 65, 67, 70
Ann V., 76
Armistead, 95
Arthur, 87
Augusta, 89
Barbee, 34, 56
Binns, 63
Blanchard, 99
Bourbon, 24, 26, 28–29, 73
Bryan K., 109
Burwell, 54–55, 112
Burwell P., 112–113
Calvin, 110
Caroline, 26, 31, 76
Catherine, 46

Charles, 46, 111
Daniel, 27, 56, 109–110
David, 83
Davis, 56, 102
Delilah, 74, 76
Edmund, Jr., 27
Edmund, Sr., 27
Edward Little John, 103
Elina, 110
Elizabeth, 15–19, 21–22, 27, 33, 47–50, 55–56, 62–63, 74–78, 80, 83–84, 87, 90, 92–93, 95, 99–103, 106, 108–111
Elizabeth Albridgton, 56
Elizabeth Ridley, 47
Elizabeth Wynne, 68
Emiline M. R., 91
Evan, 46
Evan, Jr., 46
Fannie, 67, 70
Fanning, 56, 63, 77, 83–84, 92, 94, 98, 100, 106
Fanning M., 83, 94, 100
Frances, 23, 58–61, 79, 103, 107
Frances Servant, 18, 24, 66
Francis, 12–13, 15, 17–18, 23–25, 28–51, 55–59, 61, 66–68, 70, 74–76, 79–80, 83–85, 87–89, 92, 97, 99, 101–106, 112
Francis II, 14, 30, 38–40, 43, 46
Francis III, 30, 40–43, 61
Francis, Jr., 30
Francis, Sr., 35, 57
Francis A., 46–47
Francis Albridgton, 13, 41, 46–47, 57, 93
Francis M., 24, 26, 73
Francis Nathaniel, 45
Francis Servant, 23
Frederick, 62

George, 46, 64, 67, 74, 101, 112
Hardy, 88
Harper, 110
Harry, 67
Hartwell, 84
Harwood, 19, 25, 27, 30, 34, 59–60, 63, 71, 73, 75–76, 78–82, 87–88, 90, 93, 102, 106
Lt. Harwood, 79
Maj. Harwood, 81–82
Harwood III, 78
Harwood, Jr., 79
Hasea, 107
Helen, 55, 100
Henly, 27
Henly T., Sr., 27
Henry, 8, 24, 34, 44, 55–56, 62, 74, 80, 94, 99–101, 107, 110, 112–113
Henry (CT), 94
Henry Francis, 7, 24, 67
Henry W., 108–109
Hinde, 25, 71–72
Holmes K., 86
Jack Mariah, 76
Jacob, 54–55
James, 22–23, 41, 44, 46–47, 53, 70, 86, 88, 90, 92, 95, 98, 103–105, 109–110
Dr. James, 60
Judge James, 100
James Alfred, 86, 90, 93, 103
James B., 102–103
James Cain, 106
James H., 102
James K., 100, 109
James K. II, 109
Sen. James K., 42
Sen. James K. I, 109
James Servant, 18, 23–24, 66, 69–70, 72
Jamie, 109

Jamie Eagle, 68
Jane, 55
Jemima, 41–43, 50, 52–53, 87, 95, 97–98, 106
Joel Lane, 55–56
John, 4, 13, 15, 17–18, 22–25, 28–29, 32, 34, 42, 44, 46, 54–64, 66, 70–77, 79–80, 83–84, 86–87, 89–90, 92–104, 106, 108, 111, 113
John II, 30, 46
John, Jr., 24, 34, 57–59, 63, 73, 108
John, Sr., 24, 34, 62–63, 70
John, Sr. of War.Co., 34
John A., 62, 71–73
John Allen, 68, 108
John C., 55, 76, 83–86, 91, 97, 106
Capt. John C., MD, 54
John Francis, 49
John P., 76, 91, 93, 104
John R., 41, 62, 84, 94, 100
John Ridley, 63, 83–84, 100
Dr. John Ridley, 106–107
John Sheldon, 68
John Tingnall, 93
John Wood, 67, 74
Joseph, 62
Judith, 42, 62, 78–79
Julia, 55
Kimbrough, 55–56, 68, 92, 108–109
Lavinia, 44
Lazarus, 62
Leila, 107
Leonidas, 109
Leroy, 55
Lily, 86–87, 109
Louisa E., 54–55, 112
Louisa Maria, 76
Lovick, 46

Lucy, 24, 28, 41–42, 74–75, 80, 87, 95, 99, 102, 104, 106, 109
Lucy Binns, 27
Lucy Maria, 93
Lula, 109
Lydia, 41–43, 62, 75–76, 87, 96, 102
Lydia Ann, 106
Madere, 107
Margaret, 16–17, 19–22, 27, 65, 87, 102, 107, 110
Margaret Wood, 68
Marget, 21
Maria, 80
Martha, 30, 34, 41–42, 48, 78–79, 81, 83–84, 86–90, 92, 94, 100, 102–103, 107–108
Martha, Jr., 90, 94, 100
Martha A., 80
Martha Bustian, 63, 100
Martha C., 76, 101
Martha Cary, 90
Martha Elizabeth, 109
Martha M., 90, 103
Mary, 18, 22–26, 28, 30, 34–36, 41–43, 47, 50, 56, 58–63, 66–67, 71–75, 79–81, 83–84, 86–89, 91, 94–95, 98–104, 106, 108–111
Mary Allen, 27
Mary Ann, 108
Mary B., 84, 94, 100
Mary C., 96
Mary Elizabeth Ridley, 44–45
Mary Francis Hawkins, 75
Mary H., 108
Mary K., 109
Mary Lee, 81
Mary Morris, 86
Mary P., 56, 108, 112

Mary T., 74
Matilda, 55
Matthew, 4, 7, 9, 15–19, 20–24, 26, 28–44, 47, 50–51, 55–57, 64, 65, 66, 69, 72, 74, 78–82, 85, 87–89, 91–93, 96–98, 100–103, 106–107, 109, 118
Matthew I, 10, 13–16, 20, 29–30, 33, 35, 37–39, 50, 54, 56–57, 61, 78, 80
Matthew II, 14, 17–20, 22, 26, 30–31, 34, 38, 48, 50, 64–66, 80, 95
Matthew III, 30, 39–41
Matthew IV, 30, 94, 102
Matthew of War. Co., 30, 34
Matthew, Jr., 23, 32, 75
Matthew, Sr., 14, 33, 35, 79
Capt. Matthew, 19
Matthew W., 106
Meta, 109
Mildred H., 108
Millicent, 99
Mittie, 56
Nancy, 24, 28, 55, 61, 71–73, 99–100, 103–104, 107–108, 111
Nancy Harwood, 74
Nancy T., 67, 71, 73
Nancy Timson, 64, 67
Nathaniel, 15, 17, 26, 30–31, 33, 38, 40–43, 54–56, 62, 77, 82, 87, 92, 95–100, 107–109, 111–112
Nathaniel (CT), 54, 56, 77, 94, 97
Nathaniel (WP), 55–56, 77, 94
Nathaniel II, 107
Nathaniel, Jr., 49, 52, 54–55, 77, 98
Nathaniel, Sr., 52, 56, 77, 98
Nathaniel, Sr. (CT), 98

Nathaniel, Sr. (WP), 34, 56
Nathaniel A., 55
Nathaniel K., 26, 31
Nipper, 56
Norma, 75
Oscar M., 80
Patsy, 55–56, 83, 86, 91, 100,
    108–109
Patsy E., 56
Pembroke, 62
Penelope, 63, 83–84, 91–92,
    106
Penny Hardy, 97–98
Peter H., 109
Phillip, 18, 23–24, 44, 56, 66, 72
Polly, 22, 27, 33, 55–56, 84, 107,
    110
Polly Ridly, 98
Rachel, 46, 55–56
Rachel J., 54
Rachel M., 80
Randolph, 61
Redding, 41, 55–56, 63, 76–77,
    83–84, 86, 91–92, 94,
    97–98, 100, 106
Richard B. Francis, 89
Ridley, 17, 19, 22, 41–43, 56,
    86–87, 100, 106–107
Robert, 63, 70
Robert Tignal, 93
Col. Robert Tignal, 86, 93
Roger, 46
Rufus, 109
Samuel, 32, 50, 53, 62, 106
Sarah, 22, 26–27, 31, 34, 42, 46,
    55, 62, 67, 73–74,
    83–84, 88–90, 92, 94,
    99–102, 108, 111
Sarah A., 89–90
Sarah C., 26, 66, 73
Sarah C. Allen, 26, 66, 73–74
Sarah E., 100
Sarah Elizabeth, 100
Sarah Jones Hopkins, 89

Sarah Redding, 42
Sarah Ruth, 110
Servant, 17–24, 26, 34, 59, 64–
    74, 98
Capt. Servant, 74
Maj. Servant, 24
Rev. Servant, 64–65, 69
Servant, Sr., 71–72
Serviento, 29, 74
Seth, 55–56, 92, 99, 111–112
Seth, Jr., 111
Seth, Sr., 111–112
Seth A., 111
Sidney, 109
Simon, 83
Sintha, 74
Susan, 67, 86–87, 91, 100–102,
    107, 112
Susan J., 80
T. P. Eppes Armistead, 75, 95
Temperance, 55, 112
Thomas, 19, 33, 56, 62, 75, 83–
    84, 86, 88, 91, 94
Thomas A., 81–82, 88–89
Thomas Benjamin, 87
Thomas Grant, 107
Thomas Grant, Jr., 107
Thomas Lovick, 46
Thomas Norman, 95
Tignal, 15, 17, 34, 36–37, 41–42,
    55, 69, 71, 73, 75–79,
    81–94, 97–98, 100–
    104, 106–107
Col. Tignal, 77, 83, 106
Tignal, Jr., 75, 77, 83–86, 88–92,
    94, 97
Dr. Tignal, Jr., 86
Tignal, Sr., 75, 77, 84–85, 88, 91,
    97, 101
Capt. Tignal, Sr., 88
Col. Tignal, Sr., 76
Tignal W., 85–86
Timothy, 55–56, 112
Timothy Watton, 55

Unice, 76
Vincler (or Vinkler), Jr., 74, 76
Vincler, Sr., 74–76
Vincler, 74–76, 87, 90–91, 95, 102–104
Vincler R., 76, 93
Vincler Robert, 75
Wesley, 45, 47, 55–56, 92, 101, 112
Westwood, 74–76, 87, 92, 103
Westwood A., 63, 75–76, 84, 97, 103, 106
Westwood Armistead, 74, 87
William, 18, 20, 22–25, 27, 41, 50, 52–56, 62, 64–66, 73, 75–76, 81, 88, 90, 93–98, 102–105, 108, 110
William, Jr., 25–26, 95
William, Sr., 24, 95
William B. (Hellcat Billy), 34, 64, 70, 74, 96
William E., 80
William H., 28, 67, 89–90, 96
Dr. William H., 103
William Hogan, 108
William K., 109
William M., 27
William R., 96
William Servant, 7, 26, 34, 66, 70, 74
William Servant, Jr., 26, 66–67
William Servant, Sr., 24, 66
William Westwood, 74, 95
Willis, 41, 50, 82–83, 97–99
Willis T., 55
Jordan
Elizabeth, 62

K

Kennard
Hartwell S., 107
James Blake, 107
Kimbrough
Goldman, 110
Grizeal, 56
James, 107, 110
James Edward, 109
Nathaniel, 110
Patsy, 110
Peg, 34, 56
Sarah, 26, 31, 34, 107, 109
Willis, 110
King
Hartwell, 87
John Curtis, 87
Susan, 86–87, 106
Kippin
Edward, 21

L

Lane
Joel, 55–56
John, 55, 100
Martha, 63, 83, 100, 106
Lanier
Polly, 44
Leach
John, 55
Leathers
Betsy, 76
Betsy N., 74
William, 76, 103
Lee
Fitzhugh, 108
Francis, 23, 28
Mary, 36, 74, 89, 102
Lewis
Nathaniel, 95
Robert, 90, 102
Sally, 62
Lott
John, 43
Lowry

Elizabeth Ann Sanders, 80
Lucas, 2
  Anne, 60
  Elizabeth, 58, 60
  John, 59
  John Jones, 58, 60, 63
  Lucy, 58, 60
  Nancy, 58, 60
  Robert, 18, 23, 58–61, 64, 74
  Robert, Sr., 60
  Robert Gervase, 58, 60, 63
  Sally, 58, 60
  Thomas, 58, 60
Ludwell, 2
Lyon
  Mary, 103

M

Macauley
  Helen M., 61
Mallicote
  Elizabeth, 62
  John, 15
Mann
  Thomas, 92
Mason
  T. K., 109
Massenburg
  Ann, 108
McCullers
  John, 41
McDoritt
  T. S., 109
McKnight
  Alexander, 84
McNeil
  John, 110
  Mildred, 110
  Nora, 110
  William, 110
McSwain
  C. D., 109

Eleanor, 11
Mims
  Drury, 41
Morehead, 84
  Mr., 104
Morris
  Mary, 93
Morrison
  Peggy, 62
Morton
  Harriet, 89–90
  Martha, 89–90
  Tignal J., 89, 103
Moss
  Lucy, 24, 28, 73–74
  Sheldon, 28–29
Munford
  Robert, 85
Murphy
  Dr, 83
Mutter
  Mr., 61

N

Nealson
  Robert Withe, 102
Nelson, 65
  Gen., 6
  Capt. Thomas, 68
  William, 96
Newbern
  James, 76
  Martha, 76
Newman
  Justinia, 67
  Solomon, 62
Newsom
  Julian, 47
Nicholson
  Calvin, 83, 100
Norman
  Elizabeth, 74, 95

Norment
    Lucy, 109
    Lucy Ann, 26, 31
Nowell
    Thomas, 3–4

P

Page
    Mann, 96
    Tayloe, 96
Palmer
    James, 55
    John, 55
    Mary, 54–55
    Nathaniel J., 55
Pattillo
    James A., 103
    Martha, 90
    Susan, 103
    William, 102
    William J., 90
Paxton
    Milton, 107, 110
    Polly, 34, 56
Peine
    Mary Delia, 109
Penny
    Betsy, 83
Perklinson
    Mary A., 86
Perry
    Betsy, 107
    Burwell, 45, 55–56
    Elizabeth, 107
    Rachel, 112
Phillips
    Lydia, 81
    Mary Louise, 81–82
Plant
    Frank, 110
Plummer
    Mr., 109

Pope
    Mr., 107
Portis
    Mr., 35
    George, 32
Portlock
    George, 18, 51
    Lydia Day, 18
Pott, 2
Powell
    Elizabeth, 56
    Estelle Webb, 35
    Seymour, 24, 28
Power
    Ann, 110
    Mary Kimberly, 110
    Roberta, 110
    Ruth, 110
Procer
    Grace, 16
Pulliam
    Mr., 112
    A., 55
    Amelia, 54
    John A., 54
Pyland
    Robert, 3

R

Raegan
    Ann, 109–110
Ransome
    Matthew, 83
Ravennett, 2
Richards
    William, 19
Ridgell
    Col., 9, 67
Ridley
    Anne, 63
    Catherine Ella, 63
    Elizabeth, 32

Elizabeth Day, 18
James, 18
John, 100
Louise, 63
Martha, 63
Mary, 18, 40–41, 47, 49, 63, 79, 83, 85
Nathaniel, 18, 44
Nathaniel II, 18
Thomas, 18
Robbins
Mary, 43
Roberts
Mary (Pollie), 62
Rogers
Euny, 76, 104
Roles
Catherine, 94
Rolfe, 2
Roscow
William, 15
Routon
Frances Lenora, 109
Ralph, 109

S

Salter
Eva, 67
Sanders, 2
Scasborough
Mr., 84
Mary, 76
Penny, 84
Thomas H., 76
Tignal, 84
Sclater
James, 4, 13
Rev. James, 65
Seires
Mark, 15
Semmes
Miss, 93

Servant
Bertrand, 17, 64, 69, 72
Frances, 17, 22–23, 64–65, 70, 72, 74, 102
William S., 73
Simmons
Ann, 21, 50
Elizabeth, 21–22, 50
John J., 104
Lucy, 44
Mary, 21–22, 50–51
Sledge
Paton, 97
Slocum
Anne Taylor, 110
Lt. Henry, 110
Smith
Mr., 84
Delia, 43
Frances Susan, 103
Dr. James S., 43
Jane, 18
Mary R., 43
Penny, 41, 76, 84
Richard, 76, 84, 91
Sallie M., 107
Sally McCullers, 100
Sarah E., 108
Susanna, 44–45
Snickers
Ann, 41–42, 99, 106–107
Snignall
Samuel, 9, 14
Sommerlings
Henry, 20
Southall
Albert G., 27
Frances (Jones), 3
James B., 59, 79
James Barrett, 3, 60
Mary, 27
Peyton Randolph, 3, 61
Speed
John J., 101

Rosa Ann, 102
Starkey
    Robert, 86
Stevens
    Alvin, 110
Strechen
    Ann, 101
    Lucinda, 101
Stringfield
    Anne, 62
Stuart
    Charles, 84
    Duncan, 84
    George, 41
    Mary, 78
    Tingnall, 84, 92, 107
Sumerville
    Sue, 109

T

Tabb
    John, 75
    Col. John, 75
    Mary, 24, 73, 75
    Thomas, 71, 73
Taneyhill
    John, 46
Taylor
    Temperance, 69
    Wesley, 102
    William, 90
Thompson
    Agnes, 83
    John, 102
    Margaret, 75–76, 87
Tingnal
    Mr., 37
    John, 15, 36–39, 42
    Judith, 37, 39
    Martha, 85
    Mary, 39–40, 79, 101–102
    Robert, 103

Thomas, 36, 39
Todd
    Elizabeth, 110
    Emma, 110
    Walter, 110
Trebell
    Mr., 60
Trotter
    Mr., 110
Tyler
    Judge D. G., 86, 93
    John, 103
    Mary Lyon, 103

U

Utley
    Betsy, 56

V

Vinkler (or Vincler)
    Ann, 103
    John, 75

W

Waddell
    James A., 76
    Margaret, 76, 110
Wade
    Higginson, 59
Wagstaff
    John, 36
Walker
    Jacob G., 54–55
    Laura, 55
    Rebecca, 64
Waller
    Edmund, 26
Ward
    Britan, 32

Warren
  Henry, 56
  Mary W., 56
  Mary Webb, 108
Washington
  Miss, 42
Watkins
  Benjamin, 34
  transcriber, 36
Watson
  James, 32, 35, 79
Webb
  Rev. William R., 6
Webber
  Norma, 110
Wellborn
  Charles, Jr., 107
  Judge Charles, 107
  Dorothy Lillian, 107
  Mildred, 107
Wells
  Elizabeth, 46, 99
  Emmanuel, 3
Wheeler
  Mrs. Hunter, 27
Whitaker
  Miss, 83
  Amelia Ann, 11, 40, 111
  Judge Spier, 83
  Willis, 109, 112
Whiting
  George Nathaniel, 107
  Mary, 96
Williams
  Julie, 110
  Nathaniel, 77
  Richard, 52
Wills
  Mr., 25
  John, 49, 64
  John Pate, 72
  Lucy Servant, 24
  Matthew, 24, 36, 65, 71, 73–74
  Pate, 24, 28

Thomas, 24
William, 23, 65
Wilson
  Capt., 41
  Judith, 42
  Mary, 21–22, 50, 107
  Whitaker, 109
Wissler
  Christian, 108
  J. H., 108
  Sarah, 108
Wollard
  Mrs., 57
Wood
  Bennet, 26
  Margaret Moss, 68
  Mary Ann, 34, 67, 74
  Matthew, 66, 68
Wooten
  Mr., 107, 110
  A. Ben, 34, 56
  Anna, 110
  Benjamin, 110
Wright
  Fannie Jones, 7
  J., 52
  John Turnley, 67
  Pleasant, 78
  Thomas, 3
Wurzbeck
  Emily Ann, 107

Y

Yancey
  Frances, 41, 44–45, 106
Yates
  Elizabeth Ann Upshaw, 25
Young
  Albert and Sallie, 110
  Elizabeth, 56
  Kimbrough, 110
  Norbun, 110

www.ingramcontent.com/pod-product-compliance
Lightning Source LLC
Chambersburg PA
CBHW050830160426
43192CB00010B/1972